Abortion
and Social
Responsibility

Laurie
Shrage **Abortion
and Social
Responsibility**

Depolarizing
the Debate

OXFORD
UNIVERSITY PRESS
2003

OXFORD

UNIVERSITY PRESS

Oxford   New York
Auckland   Bangkok   Buenos Aires   Cape Town   Chennai
Dar es Salaam   Delhi   Hong Kong   Istanbul   Karachi   Kolkata
Kuala Lumpur   Madrid   Melbourne   Mexico City   Mumbai
Nairobi   São Paulo   Shanghai   Taipei   Tokyo   Toronto

Copyright © 2003 by Laurie Shrage

Published by Oxford University Press, Inc.
198 Madison Avenue, New York, New York 10016

www.oup.com

Oxford is a registered trademark of Oxford University Press, Inc.

Library of Congress Cataloging-in-Publication Data
Shrage, Laurie, 1953–
Abortion and social responsibility : depolarizing the debate /
Laurie Shrage.
p.   cm. — (Studies in feminist philosophy)
Includes bibliographical references and index.
ISBN 0-19-515308-1; 0-19-515309-x (pbk.)
1. Abortion—Moral and ethical aspects—United States.
2. Abortion—Law and legislation—United States. I. Title. II. Series
HQ767.15 .S52   2003
179.7′6′0973—dc21   2002003641

9 8 7 6 5 4 3 2 1
Printed in the United States of America
on acid-free paper

To Anne Shrage

and the memory

of Bella Waldman

Preface

In the 1970s, I was reasonably optimistic that the uproar created by legal abortion would soon subside. I believed that the public would eventually get used to this newly established right just as it had adapted to mandatory integration. Thirty years later, many like me are surprised and perplexed that legal abortion continues to be a significant source of social division. I began this project several years ago with the aim of investigating the persistence of the abortion controversy in the United States. I think the explanation I develop in this book is somewhat encouraging about the prospects for positive social change.

Many feminists attribute the ongoing fight over abortion to the powerful influence of a conservative Christian movement that exploits this sensitive issue to advance reactionary political agendas. Feminist scholars and activists have shown how, in the United States, conservative Christians deploy the inflated rhetoric of "murder," "infanticide," and "genocide" to persuade Americans that the expansion of civil rights they have achieved in the last century has led their country down a path of immorality, making it a society of abortionists, perverts, and infidels. Accordingly, some scholars have studied "pro-life" organizations to assess the political and ideological methods they employ to fuel the abortion debate and render precarious the abortion rights women have won. These studies have revealed the divergent views and values underlying the abortion debate, and some have yielded strategies for countering the savvy media and political tactics of "pro-life" organizations. In brief, the thrust of feminist work on abortion in recent decades has been to challenge reactionary attacks on women's recent civil rights gains. Unfortunately, this defensive strategy may be masking some of the historical and institutional sources of the persistent and deep social divisions over abortion.

I will argue that, while conservative Christian "pro-life" organizations exploit the abortion controversy to advance their agendas, their ideologies and beliefs are not its only source. Rather, as I will try to show, the regulatory framework set out in *Roe v. Wade*, the 1973 Supreme Court decision that invalidated existing state laws on abortion, is a primary source of the continuing controversy over abortion rights in the United States. For this decision recognized a fairly broad right to abort, and not a right qualified in principled and nonarbitrary ways. The civil liberties we value, though, do not necessarily entail a relatively unrestricted right to abort. Many liberal democratic countries have made abortion legal, but virtually none acknowledges a right to abort as broad as that in the United States. In the years leading up to *Roe*, a number of different models for legal reform were proposed, debated, and enacted in particular states. Some groups sought to expand the therapeutic categories exempting doctors from criminal prosecution, and some sought abortion "on demand," that is, the repeal of the criminal laws and cumbersome regulations blocking access to safe abortions. The regulatory framework outlined in *Roe* was a significant victory for those who sought repeal rather than reform. This framework essentially gave women the right to abortion on demand for the first six months of pregnancy. Because few doctors will provide nontherapeutic abortions beyond this point, the balance *Roe* struck between a woman's privacy and the public's interest was significantly tilted toward individual rights. This balance, though, has not served the interests of all women.

Because *Roe* represented a nearly total victory for one side, rather than a compromise, and because *Roe* was and remains at odds with public opinion on abortion in the United States, there has been a predictable and forceful backlash. In the last few decades, states have found ways to get around *Roe*'s regulatory scheme in order to restrict access to abortion, such as banning the use of public funds and facilities and imposing informed consent and parental approval requirements. Moreover, the bureaucratic regulation of abortion and the sustained public controversy have contributed to a significant decrease in abortion providers. Unfortunately, these obstacles place abortion out of reach for many women, especially young, poor, and rural women. I will argue that *Roe*'s scheme is partly responsible for the public's unwillingness to ensure that all women can exercise their right to choose, in that some choices that *Roe* makes possible are widely held to be immoral. I contend that *Roe*'s regulatory scheme needs some revision, but not of the sort we got in various Supreme Court decisions a decade ago. I then propose a way to revise *Roe* that can meet the criticisms of many abortion moderates and bring its regulatory scheme more in line with public opinion. My proposal shows that there are reasonable policy options that can help to diffuse this costly fight, and that *Roe* can be modified without either being abandoned or overly constricting women's reproductive options.

The argument I make in this book is not simply about political and legal strategy. I also try to show that the minimal, libertarian regulatory structure advocated by the repeal forces is not morally and politically well justified. In chapter 1, I argue that the concept of "viability," which *Roe* employs for determining when the state may ban nontherapeutic abortions, is an ad hoc and increasingly impractical criterion for curtailing the right to abort. I investigate how the "viability" cutoff got incorporated into Blackmun's opinion, and I show that the concerns that supported its use are less relevant today and fail to take into account important factors that determine women's access to abortion services. In chapter 2, I try to show that the standard civil liberty defenses of abortion involve principles that justify only a limited right to abort. As a result, these principles do not need to be supplemented by the concept of "viability" in order to avoid justifying late-term abortions. In particular, I show that some versions of both the right-to-privacy and right-to-deny-help defenses support a qualified right to abort and are consistent with laws permitting only therapeutic abortions somewhat earlier than six months, when certain social and legal conditions are met. These conditions involve universal access to contraception and early abortion so that abortion restrictions do not single out women as a group for childcare responsibilities and violate their right to equal treatment.

In chapter 3, I consider how the proposal I have made could be taken up in campaigns for reproductive rights. I analyze various proposals by feminist scholars for countering "pro-life" propaganda, and I try to show why these proposals are impractical and capitulate to problematic assumptions about abortion. I then survey some feminist artworks on abortion that offer ways to focus the debate on questions about the social security net needed for women to have reproductive choice rather than on women simply having more "choice." I also show how the artwork of some sex worker activists can be adapted to challenge the manipulative and extremist tactics of "pro-life" groups. These groups have taken advantage of *Roe*'s unpopular and controversial character to advance an extreme agenda adverse to women's interests, and thus their public discourse needs a strong and well-conceived feminist response.

This book contributes to existing debates about how *Roe* could be rewritten and strengthened. So far this debate has focused mostly on the justificatory strategies pursued in this decision rather than the resulting regulatory framework. Though I consider which defenses of abortion rights are most fruitful, the aim of this book is to propose ways to modify the regulatory guidelines *Roe* imposed. Neither the arguments provided in *Roe*, nor those formulated after *Roe*, justify *Roe's* regulatory guidelines. If we want to diffuse the abortion debate, heal divisions, and remove regulatory policies that discriminate against young and poor women, we need not new justifications for *Roe* but some revision of its results. This book also contributes to feminist debates about why public support for abortion rights is eroding and how to rebuild support. I try to show that new approaches to regulating and defending abortion are both needed and related.

I am grateful to the College of Letters, Arts, and Social Sciences, the Center for Faculty Development, the Research and Sponsored Programs Office, and the Philosophy Department at California State Polytechnic University, Pomona for grants supporting travel, released time, equipment, and research materials. I am also grateful to the Stanford Humanities Center where I began this project during a sabbatical year four years ago. Many colleagues and friends read or heard parts of this book in progress, and their comments and suggestions helped me refine my arguments and fill out gaps in my knowledge. I would like to thank David Adams, Bruce Arnow, Janet Brodie, Susan Castagnetto, Cecilia Conrad, Nancy Cott, Jane DeHart, Wynne Furth, David Garrow, Vaughn Huckfeldt, Alison Jaggar, Linda LeMoncheck, Diana Linden, Eileen McDonagh, Judy Miles, Hilde Nelson, Linda Nicholson, Martha Nussbaum, Susan Okin, Peter Ross, Daniel Segal, Anne Shrage, Robin Sommers-Smith, Claudia Strauss, Kayley Vernalis, Roger Wertheimer, Robin West, Lora Wildenthal, the consultants at Feminist Studies, and the anonymous readers at Oxford University Press. I would also like to thank Cheshire Calhoun and Peter Ohlin for supporting this project and for all their help. The Women in Philosophy Association in Australia, the Claremont Colleges Women's Studies Program, the Women's Studies Seminar at the Huntington Library, the Association for the Study of Law, Culture and Humanities, the University of Delaware Philosophy Department, the International Association of Women Philosophers, the Southern California Philosophy Conference, the Stanford Humanities Center, the Responsibility Reading Group at Stanford University, the Philosophy Department at San Jose State University, and the Dean's Office, Philosophy Club, and Women Faculty Association at Cal Poly Pomona all provided occasions for me to share earlier drafts of this book. The work and insights of many artists made this book possible, including Ilona Granet, Carol Leigh, Barbara Kruger, Jessica Lawless, Lisa Link, and the Guerrilla Girls. I would like to thank Carol Wells and David Gabel of the Center for the Study of Political Graphics, my student research assistants Michelle Gray and Robert Ashley, the students in my Abortion seminar, and my colleagues Jerry Lerma and Wayne Rowe, for their help and suggestions. I am grateful to Hannah Segal and Nathaniel Shrage for the entertaining distractions they provided while I labored over this book.

Contents

**Abortion
and Social
Responsibility**

Is *Roe* Viable?

An Odd Scheme | Critics of *Roe v. Wade* have attributed the controversies surrounding it both to the Court's poorly justified expansion of the scope of the right to privacy and to the Court's interference with the democratic legislative process. *Roe's* defenders have responded by elaborating the privacy basis of abortion rights and by emphasizing the Court's role in protecting the civil liberties of disadvantaged groups. Since 1973, debates over *Roe* and abortion have focused primarily on the constitutional, political, and moral grounds of abortion rights and the proper role of each branch of government in contributing to the formulation of abortion law. I begin my investigation of the abortion debate by focusing not on the justifications available to defend the regulatory framework imposed by *Roe* nor on the Court's authority to impose such a framework but on the framework itself. In particular, philosophers and legal scholars have often been perplexed by the "viability" criterion that *Roe* introduced to mark the point when the government may proscribe "elective" abortions. I investigate how this concept came to be deployed in *Roe*, and I show that the concerns that led to its use are significantly less relevant in today's medical context. Though subsequent Supreme Court rulings on abortion cases have altered and weakened *Roe's* regulatory framework,[1] the concept of fetal viability has remained central to the regulation of abortion. I conclude that the viability timeframe for abortion "on demand" needs to be tossed out along with the trimester framework and that a new scheme should be devised for guiding abortion law. A new regulatory framework, and not merely a new defense of *Roe's* existing framework, is especially necessary to diffuse the backlash that has made hygienic abortion services virtually inaccessible to poor, young, and rural women. At the end of this chapter, I explore alternative criteria and mechanisms for regulating abortion. In the next chapter, I argue that the common liberal arguments employed to defend a woman's right to abort justify a right that is limited in scope and that the viability cutoff is therefore superfluous and ad hoc.

In *Planned Parenthood of Southeastern Pennsylvania v. Casey* (1992), justices Souter, O'Connor, and Kennedy, in a joint concurring opinion, wrote:

> We have seen how time has overtaken some of Roe's factual assumptions. . . . But . . . the divergences from the factual premises of 1973 have no bearing on the validity of Roe's central holding, that viability marks the earliest point at which the state's interest in fetal life is constitutionally adequate to justify a legislative ban on nontherapeutic abortions.[2]

Several years earlier in *Webster v. Reproductive Health Services*, Chief Justice Rehnquist, joined by justices White and Kennedy, wrote: "there is also no reason why the State's compelling interest in protecting potential human life should not extend throughout pregnancy rather than coming into existence only at the point of viability."[3] Rehnquist, Scalia, and Thomas favor abandoning *Roe*'s regulatory framework entirely, and "pro-choice" groups fear that, with the next retirement or two on the Court, there will be a majority of five to accomplish this. The question, though, is what regulatory guidelines will replace *Roe*'s: will we simply go back to the era when states were permitted to impose severely restrictive laws, or will the Court devise a new scheme? Sylvia Law has argued that there is a hunger for a compromise on abortion but that a reasonable compromise is unlikely because the issues underlying the debate are irreconcilable.[4] In this book, I will explore some possibilities for a satisfactory compromise, especially by exploring an alternative regulatory scheme that was considered but not adopted by the *Roe* Court. Rather than rely on the concept of "viability," this scheme allows states to restrict abortion in the second trimester to those performed for a broad set of therapeutic reasons.

Most countries that permit abortion prohibit "nontherapeutic" abortions somewhat earlier than viability—typically near the end of the first trimester. Some countries permit only therapeutic abortions but allow doctors to consider the socioeconomic hardships a pregnancy imposes in deciding the therapeutic needs of patients. Other countries have a limited period in which a woman can request an abortion for any reason. In 1975, the laws in France changed to make abortions legal for economic or social reasons "if the termination of pregnancy is performed before the end of the tenth week of gestation."[5] In 1973, Denmark changed its laws to allow abortion on demand up until twelve weeks of pregnancy.[6] India modified its laws in 1971 to permit abortions through twenty weeks of gestation that "take into account the woman's actual or reasonably foreseeable socioeconomic environment," and abortions occurring after twelve weeks with the approval of two physicians.[7] In 1978, Italy liberalized its laws to permit abortions for socioeconomic reasons during the first ninety days of pregnancy.[8] In 1986, Greece modified its laws to allow abortion on demand through the first twelve weeks of pregnancy.[9] In 1978, abortion on request became legal in Norway up until twelve weeks.[10] Since 1974, Swedish law permits abortion on request up to eighteen weeks of pregnancy.[11] In 1983, Turkey liberalized its laws to allow abortion on request through the first ten weeks.[12] Since 1979 in Cuba, both abortion and "menstrual regulation" are performed on request and for socioeconomic reasons during the first trimester, while second trimester abortions require authorization "by a committee of obstetricians, psychologists and social workers."[13] In 1973, Tunisia amended its laws to permit abortion on demand through the first three months.[14] In the United Kingdom, the Abortion Law Reform Association is currently campaigning for abortion on request for the first three months of pregnancy. Currently, the laws permit only therapeutic abortions, although physicians may consider the socioeconomic situation of the women.[15]

In her comparative study of abortion laws in twenty Western democratic countries, Mary Ann Glendon found "that when the Supreme Court established a new American abortion policy in 1973, it did so in a way which put the United States in a class by itself, at least with respect to other developed nations."[16] Glendon pointed out that the United States was unique in "forbidding *any* state regulation of abortion for the sake of preserving the fetus until viability. . . . It is alone, too, in that even after viability, it does not *require* regulation to protect the fetus."[17] *Roe*'s regulatory scheme was comparable to China's, a country in which "abortions are performed on request within six months of gestation" and that "endorses the use of abortion as a means of birth control."[18] Yet few officials or feminists in the United States would endorse the use of abortion as a primary method of population control. *Roe*'s regulatory scheme has now been modified, allowing the government to regulate abortion to advance its interest in potential life before viability, so long as the means used do not impose an "undue burden" on a woman's decision.[19] But the state may not prohibit nontherapeutic abortions before viability, meaning that women who can overcome the obstacles in their way can get abortions for any reason up to six months. Several years after *Roe*, Donald Kommers conjectured that, in reaching its decision, the Court's "interest seemed to lie in the promotion of social peace—a policy of 'live and let live'—best achieved through the constitutional right of privacy."[20] Yet, three decades later, it is quite apparent that *Roe's* policies have failed to engender social peace and instead have significantly escalated the civil war on abortion in the United States. Given the relatively unique character of *Roe's* six-month (in 1973, seven-month) window for abortion "on demand,"[21] and given that this window has contributed to a backlash that has considerably limited many women's access to abortion, we should critically evaluate the Court's reasons for adopting the viability cutoff.

The reasons for the viability cutoff are not obvious. For several decades, scholars have debated the ethical and practical relevance of fetal viability for determining the upper limit for nontherapeutic abortions. In 1984, Alan Zaitchik defended the use of viability, arguing that "it is natural to view [a viable fetus] as a person" because we can "easily *imagine* it already outside its mother's body doing well in an artificial incubator."[22] At viability then, the fetus is essentially similar to an infant except for its location. The same year, Roger Wertheimer pointed out that the Court, in *Roe*, evaded the question of when a life or person begins and does not grant the fetus the rights of a full legal person after viability.[23] Wertheimer attempted to make sense of *Roe's* use of viability by suggesting that the fetus at this stage becomes a potential human life. He writes:

> It is natural (if not necessary) to construe potentiality as linked to capability in such a way that to be a potential human life at some moment is to have the capability of living as a born human being at that moment. This, I believe, is the reasoning behind Blackmun's finding viability to be the compelling point. It has some plausibility, but I would not wish to endorse it. If it is the rationale, then little sense can be given to Blackmun's claim that the state's interest in protecting the potentiality of human life "grows in substantiality as the woman approaches term." That claim rings hollow in any case, inasmuch as that substance has no detectable legal effect prior to viability.[24]

Wertheimer rejects the notion that the capacity to be born alive renders the fetus a potential life, for there are equally good grounds for holding the fetus to be a potential life before viability. Nancy Rhoden similarly asks why the "capacity" for survival outside the womb marks a more significant fetal stage than the potential to survive if left alone, or actual survival outside the womb.[25] Some have suggested that the viability time span held force because it invokes medical factors rather than religious or metaphysical ones and the justices hoped that it would therefore be widely accepted.[26] But this rationale implies that the mere social authority of science and medicine was decisive, rather than a reasoned consideration of the moral and social relevance of the medical factors. In this chapter, I will trace the origins of *Roe*'s use of viability and explain why it was adopted by the Court for the purpose of identifying the point when state's interest in potential life becomes compelling enough to proscribe nontherapeutic abortions. I will then argue that the reasons for its adoption in 1973 do not hold up today and that we need a new approach to regulating abortion. I will propose an alternative approach, one that can come closer to achieving the aims of the justices who favored the viability cutoff.

Whence Viability? | In David Garrow's legal and social history of *Roe v. Wade*, he describes the evolution of Blackmun's opinion during the spring and fall of 1972. In a draft Blackmun circulated to his colleagues, shortly after *Roe* was reargued in the fall of that year, the line for elective abortions was drawn at the end of the first trimester. According to Garrow,

> the *Roe* draft, particularly in its two final pages, drew an extremely significant line at the end of the first trimester of pregnancy. During that first three months, Blackmun's opinion held, a state "must do no more than leave the abortion decision to the best medical judgment of the pregnant woman's attending physician." However, "For the stage subsequent to the first trimester, the State may, if it chooses, determine a point beyond which it restricts legal abortions to stated reasonable therapeutic categories."[27]

The regulatory guidelines in this draft were similar to those in the 1972 Uniform Abortion Act of the American Bar Association (ABA). This model law permitted abortions performed

> within [20] weeks after the commencement of the pregnancy [or after [20] weeks only if the physician has reasonable cause to be-

lieve (i) there is a substantial risk that continuance of the pregnancy would endanger the life of the mother or would gravely impair the physical or mental health of the mother, (ii) that the child would be born with grave physical or mental defect, or (iii) that the pregnancy resulted from rape or incest, or illicit intercourse with a girl under the age of 16 years].[28]

The ABA's scheme would have allowed state legislatures to select a point after the first trimester (i.e., around 20 weeks) when the government could require health, eugenic, or hardship grounds for performing an abortion. By stipulating an initial period in which abortions could be performed for any reason followed by a period in which abortions could be performed only for therapeutic reasons, the ABA scheme offered a compromise between repeal and reform statutes that were making their way through various state legislatures around that time.

Proponents of reform sought to expand the life-saving exception in most existing criminal statutes so that abortions could be performed when, for example, a pregnancy results from a criminal act, when it is necessary to preserve a woman's physical or mental health, when a fetal abnormality is diagnosed, or when an abortion is necessary to avoid some significant social and economic hardship. Proponents of repeal wanted existing criminal statutes to be struck down, so that a woman could obtain an abortion when her own physician was willing to perform it rather than when her case met stipulated therapeutic categories that exempted her and her doctor from criminal prosecution. Reform schemes were based on the American Law Institute's Model Penal Code and were later endorsed by the American Medical Association (AMA). Proponents of repeal argued that the reformed statutes placed too much authority in the hands of doctors and hospitals, they involved too much red tape, the exceptions were often too vague to allow doctors to understand their intent, and their enforcement would violate a woman's privacy and the privacy of the physician/patient relationship.[29]

Blackmun's final draft of *Roe* included the full text of the ABA act in a footnote, and makes reference to the act's "enlightening Prefatory Note," which says:

This Act is based largely upon the New York abortion act following a review of the more recent laws on abortion in several states and upon recognition of a more liberal trend in laws on this subject. . . . Recognizing that a number of problems appeared in

New York, a shorter time period for "unlimited" abortions was advisable. The time period was bracketed to permit the various states to insert a figure more in keeping with the different conditions that might exist among the states. . . . In addition, limitations on abortions after the initial "unlimited" period were placed in brackets so that individual states may adopt all or any of these reasons, or place further restrictions upon abortions after the initial period.[30]

The New York abortion act permitted abortion on demand until 24 weeks and had been the most radical to date. The state legislature later voted to repeal the act, but Nelson Rockefeller, the state's governor, vetoed this measure.[31] Recognizing the political turmoil New York's act produced, the ABA's model law gave state lawmakers the flexibility to choose a gestational stage for limiting abortion on demand that would be "more in keeping" with the sentiments of their constituents. Yet the regulatory scheme proposed in the final draft of *Roe* resembled the controversial New York law by marking the end of the second trimester as the point after which the state may restrict legal abortion to stated therapeutic categories, thus denying states the authority to proscribe elective abortions in the second trimester. If the Court's interest was achieving social peace, as Kommers suggests, then imposing the controversial New York scheme on the entire country was not the most obvious path to take.

Why did Blackmun switch from the ABA-type scheme in his initial draft to something closer to the New York scheme? A memo that Blackmun circulated to his colleagues just before making the switch provides the clue: "I might add that some of the district courts that have been confronted with the abortion issue have spoken in general, but not specific, terms of viability. See, for example, Judge Newman's observation in the last *Abele v. Markle* decision."[32] According to David Garrow, Justice Lewis Powell first alerted Blackmun to Judge Jon Newman's ruling, which was handed down in September 1972, just as *Roe* was about to be reargued. Garrow writes that "Powell's letter was the first intra-Court communication to put the option of extending constitutional protection for abortion choice all the way to fetal viability explicitly on the table."[33]

In *Abele v. Markle*, a case concerning a Connecticut law banning all abortions except those performed to save the life of the mother, Judge Newman writes:

The state earnestly urges upon us consideration of the situation where an abortion performed late in a pregnancy results in a "live birth." Evidence was offered to show that an aborted fetus had on occasion remained alive for several hours after an abortion operation. It is not entirely clear which of two alternative contentions the state is making: (a) that the state has a compelling interest in protecting the life of a fetus which actually survives an abortion operation; or (b) that the state has a compelling interest in protecting the life of a fetus *in utero* which has progressed to the point during pregnancy when it could survive outside the uterus.[34]

Newman then argues that the contention in (a) is valid:

If a statute protected the lives of all fetuses born alive, it would be protecting persons entitled to Fourteenth Amendment rights. And while there may be some variation in viewpoint, it would be generally accepted that the right to life of a live baby, born through survival of an abortion performed late in pregnancy, is an interest the state may protect. Moreover, a statute protecting the life of such a surviving fetus would not impair the woman's right to an abortion. The woman has had the abortion, it simply has not been successful.[35]

Newman acknowledges that the situation is somewhat different with an unborn fetus. This fetus, "for whose benefit the state interest is asserted, does not have constitutional rights."[36] According to Newman, though the state may protect entities that lack the Fourteenth Amendment protections of legal persons, the state may not protect them in a way that "would accomplish the virtually total abridgement of a constitutional right of special significance" of a legal person. Moreover, he writes, "a statute may not advance a governmental interest at the expense of a fundamental constitutional right if that interest may be advanced by a less drastic abridgement."

But Newman then explains how the state can advance its interest in protecting the unborn fetus while avoiding the near total abridgement of a woman's right to privacy. He writes,

If a statute sought to protect the lives of all fetuses which could survive outside the uterus, such a statute would be a legislative acceptance of the concept of viability. While authorities may differ on the precise time, there is no doubt that at some point during pregnancy a fetus is capable of surviving outside the uterus. And it is equally clear that there is a minimum point before which survival outside the uterus is not possible. . . . A statute designed to prevent the destruction of fetuses after viability has been reached would be subject to these considerations. Like the present statute, it would be conferring statutory rights on a fetus which does not have constitutional rights. However, the state interest in protecting the life of a fetus capable of living outside the uterus could be shown to be more generally accepted and, therefore, of more weight in the constitutional sense than the interest in preventing the abortion of a fetus that is not viable. . . . Finally, and most important, such a statute would not be a direct abridgement of the woman's constitutional right, but at most a limitation on the time when her right could be exercised.[37]

In this passage, Newman makes the leap from (a) to (b). Although the unborn fetus is not a legal person, Newman claims that, at viability, the state's interest in protecting the fetus has greater weight and that, by protecting the fetus at this stage, the government does not too drastically infringe a woman's constitutional right. When the state protects an infant who survives an abortion procedure by restricting what the doctor or woman may do to it, the state does not totally abridge a woman's constitutional right because she "has had the abortion." When the state protects a fetus who has some chance of surviving an abortion procedure, by proscribing nontherapeutic abortions, the state does not totally abridge a woman's constitutional right because it only restricts the time when she can have her abortion. And, presumably, restricting abortion at viability does not too drastically limit the time a woman has to exercise her right and therefore does not too drastically infringe her constitutional right. Yet Newman does not explain why restricting abortion after viability is not too drastic a time limit or why it might be generally accepted that the state's interest in protecting the life of the fetus becomes more compelling at viability.

After referring his colleagues to Newman's opinion, and receiving their feedback, Blackmun revised his *Roe* draft, resulting in the final draft. In response to suggestions from justices Thurgood Marshall and William Brennan, Blackmun identified two points at which the state's interests become sufficiently compelling to intrude upon a woman's privacy: after the first trimester to protect the mother's health and after viability to protect potential human life.[38] This change reflected Blackmun's willingness to revise his original scheme at the urging of his more liberal colleagues "if it could command a court."[39] And indeed the majority of the justices on the majority side in *Roe* approved the switch to viability as the point when the state could prohibit nontherapeutic abortions.

But why did they? In other words, though the Newman ruling explains where they got the concept of viability, it does not explain the judicial "acceptance of the concept of viability," to paraphrase Newman. Although Newman's ruling would permit states to prohibit nontherapeutic abortions at viability, it doesn't entirely resolve the issue of whether the state has a compelling interest in protecting the fetus before viability and whether imposing the cutoff at, say, three or five months would too drastically infringe a woman's right. One memo from Blackmun shows that, after Powell urged the Newman approach, Blackmun continued to prefer his earlier scheme. Although his initial scheme permitted states to adopt a cutoff for abortion on demand at twelve weeks, he pointed out that more liberal states could nevertheless adopt a later cutoff.[40] As a result, by adopting this scheme, the Court would be seen as less activist and more respectful of the legislative process and citizens' democratic rights.[41] His earlier scheme also addressed the concerns that many physicians apparently had about the availability of hospital facilities for second trimester elective abortions. So what advantages did the viability approach have over Blackmun's initial scheme?

The memo in which Blackmun mentions Newman's ruling provides some hints. He writes:

> One of the members of the Conference has asked whether my choice of the end of the first trimester, as the point beyond which a state may appropriately regulate abortion practices, is critical. He asks whether the point of viability might not be a better choice.
>
> The inquiry is a valid one and deserves serious consideration. I selected the earlier point because I felt that it would be more easily accepted (by us as well as others) and because most medical statistics and statistical studies appear to me to be centered there. Viability, however, has its own strong points. It has logical and biological justifications. There is a practical aspect, too, for I am sure that there are many pregnant women, particularly younger girls, who may refuse to face the fact of pregnancy and who, for one reason or another, do not get around to medical consultation

until the end of the first trimester is upon them, or, indeed, has passed.[42]

David Garrow tells us that Marshall quickly responded to this memo, endorsing the "practical aspect" of extending abortion on request to viability.[43] Mark Tushnet, Marshall's law clerk, who drafted Marshall's response, writes: "My recollection is that the letter was only one among a number of communications Blackmun received, urging him to accommodate the 'practical aspect' of the abortion problem. . . . Perhaps, however, the fact that the precise suggestion came from Marshall mattered to Blackmun."[44] With the recent release of Powell's papers, Garrow has now illuminated Powell's role, and that of Powell's law clerk, Larry Hammond, in emphasizing the practical aspects of viability.[45] These documents suggest that Powell is the "member of the Conference" referred to in Blackmun's memo here.

The journalists Bob Woodward and Scott Armstrong provide another account of the backstage maneuvering that took place among the justices at this time. They claim that Marshall worried that a twelve-week cutoff would not be feasible because "many women, particularly the poor and undereducated, would probably not get in touch with a doctor until some time after the first 12 weeks. A woman in a rural town might not have access to a doctor until later in pregnancy."[46] Whereas Blackmun and Powell mention the needs of young women,[47] Marshall apparently thought the later cutoff better protected the interests of poor, undereducated, and rural women. Woodward and Armstrong further elaborate Marshall's thinking about viability as follows: "If viability were the cut-off point, it would better protect the rural poor. Clearly, viability meant one thing in Boston, where there were fancy doctors and hospitals. There, a fetus might be sustained [after] only a few months. But in rural areas with no hospitals and few, if any, doctors, viability was probably close to full-term, or late in the third trimester."[48] This reconstruction of Marshall's thought suggests that Marshall saw viability not as stage determined in reference to the best medical technologies and successes but as one determined by the actual care facilities available to each woman. Using "viability" in this sense, women unable to get or seek medical attention would generally have more time to get abortions than socially privileged women, for the fetuses of those with less access to medical care would be "viable" later in pregnancy.

Yet, Marshall's alleged understanding of "viability" varies from how the concept came to be understood and deployed. As Alan Zaitchik explains,

> clearly enough those who want to assign moral significance to viability do not want viability to depend upon morally arbitrary factors such as geography or socioeconomic status. No one would want to say that by flying from Cambridge to Calcutta a woman suddenly gained the right to destroy a formerly "viable" but now "pre-viable" fetus, or that the fetus suddenly ceased to be a person or human, or that it suddenly lost a "right to life." So when we say that a viable fetus is one which could be saved through artificial means, given the current "state of available medical technology" . . . we do not mean medical technology *actually available* to the particular fetus in question; we mean medical technology *in principle* available, perhaps only somewhere else in the world and only to the wealthy.[49]

If Woodward and Armstrong are correct, then Zaitchik's "we" does not include Marshall, who exerted considerable influence on the use of viability in *Roe*. On Marshall's understanding of viability, the worry expressed by many abortion rights supporters—that viability will keep moving earlier in a pregnancy as medical knowledge and technology improve—is less serious. For if viability varies with a woman's actual access to advanced medical care, rather than hypothetical access, then women who would have the shortest time span to arrange abortions would presumably have the greatest access to medical care, and thus a greater ability to arrange an early abortion. Conversely, the women who would be less likely to arrange first-trimester abortions would also presumably have less access to fancy hospitals with good neonatal care, giving them a longer time span to arrange abortions.[50] Perhaps factors such as geography and socioeconomic status are not morally arbitrary for regulating abortion, as Zaitchik claims, especially if we consider how the time a woman needs to exercise her constitutional rights may vary according to these factors. Zaitchik rashly assumes that it's less morally arbitrary for the "viable" fetus's moral standing to shift with changing technology than with diverse social conditions.

Both in the preceding memo and in the Court's opinion, Blackmun calls attention not only to the practical importance of viability but to its "logical and biological justifications." Commenting on Blackmun's claims, Roger Wertheimer writes that "the mind boggles when Blackmun tells us that the holding has multiple justifications, one logical and one biological. Neither the principles of logic nor the facts of biology could individually yield a justification."[51] Critics of *Roe* have argued that the viability cutoff is morally arbitrary because it reflects neither the fetus's acquisition of important human or person attributes nor its actual separation from a woman's body but only the capacity for separate existence if the fetus should happen to be born. Because this capacity is a function of both society's medical and technological sophistication and the fetus's physiological development (especially lung development so it can survive on a respirator), viability becomes a shifting and morally irrelevant basis on which to assign a right to protection.[52] As some critics ask, why should the capacity to survive outside the womb with adequate neonatal care provide a reason to prohibit a woman from obtaining an abortion rather than the capacity to survive inside the womb with adequate prenatal care? Furthermore, as Nancy Rhoden points out, physicians generally fail to agree on how high the chances of survival must be for a fetus to be regarded as "viable," and estimates of fetal age or lung capacity, which are correlated with viability, are often imprecise.[53] Judge Newman seems to have anticipated such problems and writes, "The issue might well turn on whether the time period selected could be shown to permit survival of the fetus in a generally accepted sense, rather than for the brief span of hours and under the abnormal conditions illustrated by some of the state's evidence."[54] In sum, the apparent moral irrelevance of viability for restricting abortion and its vagueness as a biological concept show that the logical and biological justifications for viability are far from obvious. This makes it difficult to understand the judicial acceptance, or the *Roe* majority's adoption, of the concept of "viability."

Some scholars defend the use of fetal viability for regulating abortion but argue that it should mark the point when abortion is permitted, not restricted. For example, Heather Gert asks: "Isn't it odd to give as a justification for requiring a pregnant woman to support a fetus the fact that it could be supported by others?"[55] Gert argues that it is more logical to allow, rather than prohibit, pregnancy termination at viability, as long as the abortion is performed in a way that would be conducive to the fetus's survival. If viability designates the stage when the fetus is capable of surviving outside a woman's body, then, at this stage, the state need not infringe a woman's constitutional right in order to protect the fetus's life. For the state can protect a viable fetus by simply requiring a woman to cooperate with the efforts of others who wish to care for her about-to-be-ejected fetus, rather than by proscribing abortion and compelling her to gestate it. Gert writes, "To grant the State the right to protect a viable fetus is not the same as granting the State the right to require a pregnant woman to carry or subsequently care for that fetus. It never follows from the fact that the State has a certain interest that there are no restrictions on the ways in which it may protect that interest."[56] As Newman argued, in deciding among alternative means for advancing a state interest, the state should choose the one that involves "a less drastic abridgement" of citizens' constitutional rights. Unlike Newman, Gert concludes that the state should therefore allow a woman to have her abortion after viability and should only regulate the abortion method used, as well as the fetus's subsequent treatment.

Newman never explains why the state may protect fetuses that could be born alive by banning nontherapeutic abortion. He simply argues that when the state does this, it does not too drastically invade a woman's privacy. Yet Gert argues that the state can design a statute "to prevent the destruction of fetuses" with a less severe infringement. Newman also doesn't explain why the state may protect a viable fetus but not a nearly viable fetus—say, a five-month fetus. It could be argued that five months provides an ample amount of time for a woman to have an abortion. If banning abortion at six months does not too drastically abridge a woman's right, then banning abortion at five months similarly does not too drastically abridge her right, and the earlier cutoff further advances the state's interest in protecting potential life. In other words, the reasons Newman provides for permitting the state to ban abortions at viability either are not sufficient to support banning abortion at all, but only particular abortion methods, or they are sufficient to support banning abortion at viability, and possibly earlier. Newman assumes "that the state interest in protecting the life of a fetus capable of living outside the uterus could be shown to be more generally accepted and, therefore, of more weight in the constitutional sense than the interest in preventing the abortion of a fetus that is not viable,"[57] but the reactions to Roe show that this assumption is not generally accepted.

Nancy Rhoden explains why the state's interest in protecting the life of a viable fetus is greater than the nonviable fetus, and why the state's interest can only be advanced by proscribing elective abortions, rather than particular abortion methods, at this stage. The explanation has to do with the "live-birth problem," or the treatment of infants that survive an abortion procedure, which Newman's ruling addresses. Rhoden points out that the prospect of a live birth occurs only at viability and not before, and live births following an "abortion" raise difficult medical and moral issues for physicians and for society. For although others may care for and sustain the life of a fetus after viability, the health of an infant whose birth is induced prematurely, when there is no medical need to do so, may be significantly compromised. According to Rhoden, premature newborns "face a staggering array of medical problems."[58] Premature birth often results in severe physical and mental disabilities, such as loss of hearing, vision, and mental capacities, which last throughout an individual's life.[59] Consequently, statutes permitting nontherapeutic, induced premature deliveries after viability, as Gert's proposes, would result in the birth of damaged infants, even with current standards of neonatal care. Rhoden writes that "intentionally inducing an extremely premature delivery in the absence of maternal health reasons would be malpractice of the grossest kind, and the occasional live birth from late abortion creates medical and ethical dilemmas of a harrowing nature."[60] Rhoden argues that "if a society wishes to avoid the dilemmas posed by fetuses who survive abortions, then it must prohibit abortions when there is some probability the fetus could survive the procedure."[61] In sum, it is because of the possibility for live but premature births, and the moral, medical, and legal issues they raise, that the state's interest in protecting the viable fetus is, as Newman contends, "generally" accepted (at least by legally vulnerable physicians, and lawyers who look after their interests, such as Blackmun).[62] Moreover, the state cannot further its interest in potential life by a means less drastic than proscribing elective abortions that could result in a live birth.

Gert anticipates objections like Rhoden's, and addresses them by stipulating that "viability" should be understood as the point when "it is reasonably likely that [the fetus] will survive outside its mother's womb without suffering a serious handicap as a result of its removal."[63] However, with this stipulation, viability would probably occur at near term. So by changing the meaning of "viability" from capacity for mere survival after premature birth to capacity for survival with little damage, Gert's proposal in practice would be equivalent to banning nontherapeutic abortions from roughly six months to near term. Furthermore, should neonatal care for "premies" become medically comparable to delivery-at-term, a society would need to consider the costs, especially healthcare costs, of adopting policies permitting women, without medical grounds, to prematurely deliver infants who would require lengthy hospital stays in intensive care units. Unfortunately, Gert fails to do this. Gert leaves open the moral question of whether viable infants resulting from elective premature pregnancy terminations must be kept alive by others, and thus leaves open the possibility that the state could permit hospitals and physicians to deny treatment if the costs were not assumed by others voluntarily. Thus if women were permitted to terminate their pregnancies when, with the best medical care, the outcome would be the same as continuing to term, but without provisions ensuring that others will provide the best medical care, then society would face the prospect of some "aborted" premature neonates getting left untreated, or left to die. Perhaps Gert is proposing that the state should restrict the abortion method used in cases when there are others willing to care for the fetus and, in cases when there aren't, the state either should not permit a post-viability abortion, or allow the doctor or woman to choose a method not conducive to the fetus's survival.

Rhoden's arguments make evident society's need to proscribe nontherapeutic abortions after viability, but they do not fully explain why the government should not ban nontherapeutic abortion before viability. Although before viability the live-birth problem does not arise, which avoids the treatment dilemmas faced by doctors and society, there are other moral issues to face. For example, some oppose nontherapeutic abortion when the fetus is capable of feeling pain. Thus, one might maintain that the state's interest in protecting the viable fetus is greater than the nonviable fetus, and also hold that the state's interest in protecting the sentient fetus is greater than the nonsentient fetus. A regulatory scheme that restricted abortion to stated therapeutic categories around the time of sentience would further this interest. In short, although the live-birth problem explains the appeal of restricting abortion after viability, it does not completely explain why the *Roe* Court chose not to restrict nontherapeutic abortions before viability, as Blackmun's initial scheme would have allowed. That is, the justices might have gone with a scheme promoted by the reformers rather than the repeal advocates, one that permitted states to limit abortions somewhere in the second trimester to a set of therapeutically defined practices. Such schemes would have given women some amount of time for unrestricted abortion, thus not "too drastically" infringing their constitutional right, while advancing the state's interest in protecting potential life. Under a reform-type scheme, some states probably would have restricted abortions significantly in the second trimester, and others might have left abortion relatively unrestricted until viability or until birth. The reason the Court went with a repeal scheme rather than a reform scheme has to do with the privacy justification given in *Roe* and the concerns I mentioned earlier about the workability of reformed laws.

Before *Roe*, most state statutes prohibiting abortion allowed for some therapeutic exceptions, especially abortions "necessary to preserve a woman's life," and some statutes included "health." At least two of these laws were struck down by lower courts on the grounds that this language was vague. Given the room for professional disagreement over the therapeutic necessity of an abortion, a doctor who might interpret these exceptions broadly could be subject to prosecution if the courts decided to interpret these exceptions narrowly. Thus abortion laws could be held to violate the right of doctors to practice medicine in accordance with their own best judgment or expertise. Infringing this right not only subjected doctors to the arbitrary authority of the state but it also could inhibit the delivery and progress of medical care. Yet, before ruling on *Roe*, the Supreme Court struck down one of the lower court rulings decided on vagueness grounds, writing that "so long as 'health' was correctly understood as including 'psychological as well as physical well-being,'" abortion laws could be applied by physicians without risk of prosecution. In other words, state laws prohibiting all abortions except therapeutic ones were constitutional only if the exceptions they permitted were given the widest possible interpretation so that doctors would not be second-guessed by courts and law enforcers.[64] As *Roe* was being argued before the Court, the justices considered whether the Texas abortion law should be struck down on vagueness grounds. But the justices were divided in regard to the various vagueness rulings.

When it became apparent to the justices in favor of invalidating the Texas law that there was a majority for striking it down on privacy grounds, an apparent "conceptual difficulty" arose. The Court faced the issue of whether the state could override a woman's fundamental right to privacy at any point in a pregnancy to protect an entity that was not a legal person. That is, acceptance of the idea that a woman's right to privacy encompassed the decision to abort seemed inconsistent with any government prohibition of abortion, even late-term nontherapeutic ones. If a woman has a fundamental right to privacy, then what state interest is sufficiently compelling to limit her exercise of this right to the first or second trimester? Laws restricting abortion, even with therapeutic exceptions, invade a woman's constitutionally protected privacy and the privacy of the doctor-patient relationship, and protecting the interests of a nonperson might not be sufficiently compelling to justify this invasion. Yet the justices did not want to conclude that any ban on abortion before birth would be unconstitutional.

Newman's ruling, which struck down the Connecticut abortion law on privacy grounds, showed the Court how privacy reasoning could be consistent with a ban on nontherapeutic abortions after the point of viability. As Powell argued in a letter to Blackmun, "once we take the major step of affirming a woman's constitutional right, it seems to me that viability is a more logical and defensible time for identifying the point at which the state's overriding right to protect potential life becomes evident." According to Garrow, Powell closed this letter "by again mentioning that he was 'favorably impressed' with how Jon Newman had 'identified viability as the critical time from the viewpoint of the state.'"[65] Powell held that the viability cutoff for abortion on demand reflected sufficient respect for a woman's right to privacy in procreative matters. Although proscribing nontherapeutic abortions at viability invades a woman's privacy, it involves less of an invasion than Blackmun's original cutoff. Moreover, because of the medical, ethical, and legal issues raised by the prospect of live births following an abortion, few doctors would perform elective abortions after viability; thus bans on nontherapeutic abortions after viability would not too severely limit a woman's right to be let alone. Furthermore, the viability timeframe appeared to yield another advantage. Powell's clerk, Larry Hammond, had pointed out that by invoking the idea of viability to mark the cutoff rather than "any specific point in time," the Court would not be appearing to act as "super legislature."[66] Shortly after *Roe*, Lawrence Tribe argued that, by using viability, the court structured "the process of change in constitutional principles without dictating end products."[67] Liberal justices such as Marshall and Brennan preferred the longer time span for unrestricted abortion, as I mentioned, because they thought it better protected the interests of poor, rural, and young women. In sum, "viability" helped Blackmun solve the conceptual challenge of identifying a point when the state could curtail a woman's fundamental constitutional right, and it bridged the differences between the liberal justices who wanted few restrictions and their conservative colleagues on the Court. Moreover, the viability cutoff seemed to reflect judicial principles rather than a legislative compromise.

However, invoking the idea of "viability" to mark the cutoff for nontherapeutic abortions, rather than identifying a particular week, did little to stall the charge that the Court acted legislatively. In 1975, Alexander Bickel wrote: "In the place of the various state abortion statutes in controversy and in flux, the Supreme Court prescribed a virtually uniform statute of its own."[68] Bickel's observation alludes to the controversy over the New York statute and to statutes significantly more moderate than New York's, some of which had failed to gain approval in other states. Because the Court's ruling held as constitutional only statutes virtually equivalent to the New York scheme, its prescription of a "virtually uniform statute" was troubling even to moderates on this issue. In 1996, Cass Sunstein, a strong defender of abortion rights for women, wrote:

> It would not be especially hard to reach the conclusion that laws forbidding abortion are constitutionally troublesome. . . . But— and this is an important qualification—it does not follow that the Supreme Court was correct to invalidate such laws in 1973 in *Roe v. Wade*. The Court would have done far better to proceed slowly and incrementally, and on grounds that could have gathered wider social agreement and thus fractured society much less severely. The Court might have ruled that abortions could not be prohibited in cases of rape or incest, or that the law at issue in *Roe* was invalid even if some abortion restrictions might be acceptable. Such narrow grounds would have allowed democratic processes to proceed with a degree of independence—and perhaps find their own creative solutions acceptable to many sides.[69]

Blackmun's initial scheme, compared to his revised scheme, would have provided more room for democratically elected state legislators to find creative solutions acceptable to larger constituencies.

Furthermore, *Roe*'s viability timeframe has done little to protect the interests of young and poor women.[70] For conservative states and state legislators, offended by the wide window for abortion on demand, soon responded by cutting off public funds and facilities for all abortions, including most therapeutic ones, in both the first and second trimesters. A wide window for unrestricted abortion, but without public funding for healthcare that includes abortion, puts hygienic abortion services beyond the reach of many poor, young, or geographically isolated women. The idea of abortion "on demand," or abortion as a woman's "choice," had been controversial, even when the timeframe proposed was much shorter. After *Roe*, state legislators reasoned that the government need not remove obstacles not of its own making to ensure that all women can make their own "choice."

In short, the viability time span for nontherapeutic abortions did little either to help women who are socially disadvantaged or to repel criticism of the Court for interfering with the democratic political process. Furthermore, with changes in the medical procedures used for abortions, doctors today face different treatment dilemmas when performing abortions after viability. In particular, because new abortion techniques can eliminate the possibility of live birth, the harrowing treatment dilemmas and professional conflicts Rhoden describes no longer need arise. However, these new procedures raise other harrowing practical and moral issues that the viability cutoff fails to address. I will discuss some of these dilemmas below.

Viability as a Proxy Criterion | In 1986, Nancy Rhoden pointed out that denying abortions to their patients after viability was not the only means doctors could use to avoid inducing a potentially damaging premature delivery. For a doctor can choose an abortion procedure virtually guaranteed to cause the fetus's death, even on an otherwise viable fetus. For example, a delivery induced with saline rather than prostaglandin, or some combination of both, is more likely to result in fetal death. Rhoden claims that "some physicians advocate injecting digoxin into the fetus' heart to cause cardiac arrest *in utero*" to bring about fetal death.[71] Because doctors can use methods in late pregnancy that are reasonably certain to result in fetal death, prohibiting abortion after viability is not the only way a society can avoid the dilemmas of "abortions" that produce live births. The government could simply permit doctors to perform guaranteed feticidal pregnancy terminations after viability, as they are now allowed to do before viability.

Like the live-birth problem, such procedural options, though, raise serious moral and practical questions. Should a woman or doctor be allowed to choose a guaranteed feticidal method after viability and, if so, under what circumstances? The courts have ruled that: "After viability, if two methods are equally safe for the woman, the state constitutionally can require that the one least hazardous for the fetus be used."[72] The adoption of laws proscribing feticidal abortion procedures after viability, when these procedures offer no therapeutic advantage over other methods, is likely to increase the numbers of live births following postviability abortions, though the percentage of abortions at this stage is quite low. When alternative abortion methods pose different levels of risk to a woman, the courts have ruled that the state may not require a physician to make trade-offs between the woman's health and the fetus's survival, even after viability. Thus when a feticidal method of pregnancy termination is safer for a women, she or her physician may choose that method, even after viability (in a therapeutic abortion).

In a recent ruling striking down a Nebraska law banning so-called partial birth abortions, the Supreme Court reaffirmed the principle that the law must not require a woman (or her doctor), either postviability or previability, to use a procedure that is less safe for her.[73] The Nebraska law aimed to prohibit a procedure called "Dilation and Extraction" (D & X) in which a physician removes an intact fetus through a woman's dilated cervix by collapsing the fetus's skull. Because the fetus's body is "delivered" through the cervix first (supposedly resulting in a "partial birth"), opponents regard the procedure as a form of infanticide. This procedure and a related procedure, "Dilation and Evacuation" (D & E), in which the fetus is destroyed in the uterus and may be removed in pieces, are currently performed in the late second trimester, but before viability. Both D & X and D & E are guaranteed feticidal abortion methods, and they are generally regarded as safer for a woman than induced expulsion via an injection of a drug that causes uterine contractions. This is because of the potential side effects of the drugs used to induce labor and because, with D & X or D & E, the cervix does not need to be dilated as much as with induced labor and delivery. The new late-term procedures may even pose lower medical risks than ordinary (i.e., not drug-induced) labor and childbirth. Importantly, once doctors are able to perform abortions using the methods of D & X and D & E beyond weeks 23 or 24 with fewer medical risks than childbirth, then the guideline that the state can prohibit abortions after viability, except in cases where it is necessary to preserve a woman's life or health, stops being meaningful. For then arguably any abortion performed by D & X or D & E could be said to be necessary to preserve a woman's health by allowing her to avoid the greater health risks of labor and delivery, or caesarean section.[74]

When the court struck down the Nebraska law, which aimed to prohibit D & X, it reasoned that just as the state may not prohibit a safer abortion method postviability, it may not do so previability. So if a method that would induce a stillbirth is safer for the woman than one that would produce a live birth, it must be allowed. Similarly, if D & X is safer for a woman than D & E or both are safer than induced child-birth, then they must be allowed. In the current medical context (the context of *Stenberg*), there is usually little medical advantage for a woman in a healthy pregnancy to induce a live birth or stillbirth prematurely, and D & X and D & E are generally performed before viability. Yet if in the future D & X (or D & E) can be performed after viability with lower medical risks than labor and delivery (or a Caesarean section), either because D & X (or D & E) can be performed later or because viability moves earlier, then the legal justification for regulating abortion will be less clear. The *Roe* Court held there was no need to regulate abortion in the first trimester to protect women's health, given that the standard procedures (D & E and now RU 486) are safer than childbirth. And they saw no compelling reason to prohibit nontherapeutic abortion before the stage when doctors will not perform them (to avoid the live-birth problem). Yet when D & X or D & E can be used for abortions in the last third of pregnancy, some doctors may be willing to use them, given that there is no risk of live birth. By proscribing abortions in this medical context, the state will neither be furthering its interest in protecting women's health nor its interest in preventing harm to fetuses that could potentially survive. In *Akron v. Akron Center for Reproductive Health* (1983), O'Connor wrote in her dissent:

> The Roe framework . . . is clearly on a collision course with itself. As the medical risks of various abortion procedures decrease, the point at which the State may regulate for reasons of maternal health is moved further forward to actual childbirth. As medical science becomes better able to provide for the separate existence of the fetus, the point of viability is moved further back toward conception.[75]

In 1986, Nancy Rhoden claimed that "With the latest figures showing abortion safer than childbirth even after week 21 . . . the collision of trimesters of which Justice O'Connor warned is close upon us."[76] Although viability has not moved much earlier in the last decade or so, "the point at which the State may regulate for reasons of maternal health" has probably moved beyond viability toward childbirth, because the medical risks of late abortion procedures have decreased. Therefore, the state can only promote its interest in protecting potential life, at any stage of pregnancy, by compelling pregnant women to assume the medical risks of childbirth, which are higher than those now involved in most abortions. And, given that the procedures that are safer for women than labor and delivery carry no risk of live birth—a risk that made the state's interest in potential life compelling at viability—the state's interest in avoiding harm to fetuses that could survive, as well as all the resulting treatment dilemmas, is no longer relevant.

Nevertheless, while new late abortion methods may be safer for women than labor and delivery and may avoid producing orphaned and potentially damaged neonates requiring highly expensive care, the prospect of women having feticidal abortions at seven, eight, or nine months into healthy pregnancies is not attractive. And the lack of comfort some have with using D & X late in a healthy pregnancy probably has little to do with the fetus's viability. Many object to feticidal abortions late in a healthy pregnancy not because the fetus is capable of some sort of extrauterine existence but simply because, by late pregnancy, fetuses seem to acquire many important human characteristics that would make their intentional destruction, without substantial cause, tragic. Viability may have had some moral relevance when abortions after viability could result in unanticipated live births and were generally equal to or greater than childbirth in risk. However, in the current medical context this is not the case. So if society wants to restrict elective fetal destruction and abortion at some point in a pregnancy, judges and legislators will need criteria other than viability.

To locate the point at which the state may invade a woman's privacy to advance its interest in potential life, it is not necessary to invoke a concept such as "viability." Instead, our laws can designate a point along the continuum of change that pregnancy involves. Our laws do this frequently, when for example they stipulate a minimum age for driving, voting, or drinking. While some people have the maturity earlier than the minimum age to drive, vote, or drink responsibly and some may lack it years beyond the minimum age, these laws offer cutoff points that appear to work for most individuals.[77] We don't need to imagine that, when a person turns eighteen, some critical stage of "maturity" has been reached in order to justify the rights and privileges she gains at this age. Similarly, we don't need to imagine that, when a fetus reaches some number of weeks, some critical change takes place in a fetus or a pregnancy that justifies social protection or the right to continued support for the fetus. We only need to hold that at some number of weeks the fetus has reached a stage of development that renders it similar enough to other beings that have this right or privilege. In the next chapter, I will argue that neither privacy-based nor equality-based justifications require that the right to unrestricted abortion be as broad as six months. Moreover, none of these defenses requires that the right to unrestricted abortion be limited by some fetal capacity such as viability.

Although Rhoden recognizes the ways in which the concept of "viability" has become morally irrelevant, she argues for retaining viability to mark the upper limit for unrestricted abortion. But she claims that we need to distinguish two aspects of the meaning of "viability"— technological survivability and a stage occurring in late gestation—and she favors deemphasizing the former and focusing on the latter aspect of its meaning.[78] Rhoden describes different hypothetical medical contexts in order to demonstrate that a continued emphasis on survivability will lead to unintuitive legal results. For example, should technological survivability become possible in the first trimester, or for some bizarre reason become no longer possible until nine months, emphasizing survivability would generate timeframes for abortion on demand that are either too short to be practical or too long to be ethically comfortable. To avoid these unacceptable results, Rhoden urges courts to ignore this component of the meaning of "viability" and instead to emphasize the symbolic association of viability with late gestation. She then attempts to locate a point at the onset of late gestation that will allow a woman ample time to make and execute a decision about an unplanned pregnancy or a pregnancy involving a disabled fetus—a point that sufficiently respects a woman's right to privacy. However, Rhoden is unable to locate a cutoff that would work in almost all cases (including a late diagnosis of a severely disabling and untreatable fetal condition), and she suggests a number of possible soft cutoffs that could be eased in extreme cases.

Rhoden seems to assume, like many repeal advocates, that the cutoff for unrestricted abortion should be late enough to encompass abortions that are sought for medical or socioeconomic hardship. Yet her soft cutoffs, which are eased in extreme cases, suggest a scheme in which the period for abortion on demand is wide enough to encompass cases involving no specific medical hardship or other unanticipated need and in which abortions that meet various stipulated exceptions are permitted beyond that period.[79] A scheme with a cutoff for unrestricted abortion that works for most women in nonextreme cases but allows for exceptions in extreme cases communicates to women that they are expected to arrange abortions as early as possible. Although the approval process for therapeutic abortions under such schemes can become cumbersome, it is easier to address this problem than to find a cutoff point for unrestricted abortions short of birth that will work for women in extreme situations. Moreover, if the rationale for keeping the viability timeframe is that it offers the best protection against the arbitrary implementation of moderate schemes, three decades after *Roe* it is clear that repeal schemes cannot prevent the creation of bureaucratic hurdles. Shortly after *Roe*, Judith Blake warned scholars that the discrepancy between the Court's ruling and public opinion could encourage forms of political, professional, and bureaucratic resistance that would determine "whether abortion is elective to the extent allowed by *Roe* . . . or, for significant segments of the population, prohibited on a de facto basis."[80] *Roe*'s six-month upper limit for unrestricted abortion was in 1973, and still remains, considerably at odds with American public opinion.[81] Although some may have hoped public opinion would change over time, thirty years later we see that Blake's warning was rather prescient. *Roe*'s controversial regulatory guidelines have brought on a storm of state laws imposing bureaucratic hurdles, so that today abortion has become a class privilege rather than each woman's right. A more moderate reform-type scheme with reasonable therapeutic requirements in the second trimester might have preempted much of the political, professional, and bureaucratic resistance to *Roe* that Blake rightly predicted, as well as its unfortunate class effects.

States have been successful in subverting *Roe*'s scheme, in part, because the Supreme Court, loaded with anti-*Roe* judges, has replaced the "strict scrutiny" test (generally applied to infringements of fundamental rights) with the "undue burden" standard, thereby diminishing the force of the privacy argument made in *Roe*.[82] Poor, young, and geographically isolated women probably would have fared better under Blackmun's original twelve-week limit for nontherapeutic abortions. For under *Roe*'s scheme, the federal and state governments have resorted to withdrawing public funds and imposing parental approval and "informed consent" requirements in order to limit access to abortion on demand—requirements likely to disproportionately affect poor, working-class, young, and rural women. Moreover, the controversial nature of abortion on demand, combined with an explosion of bureaucratic restrictions, has contributed to a significant decrease in physician providers, which has especially hurt poor, young, and rural women.[83] Unfortunately, these women are not free to choose among the available providers. Had states been allowed to impose therapeutic requirements in the second trimester, as under Blackmun's initial scheme, there would have been less of a need to impose the kind of restrictions that discriminate on the basis of class or age. Although repeal advocates fear that transferring authority to doctors will work against women's interests, this need not be the case, especially if there is some social solidarity between doctors and women or if there is a fair appeal process when a woman's request is turned down.[84] Repeal advocates who feared that reform schemes could be applied in an arbitrary fashion by doctors, depending on their sympathies, should acknowledge that the bureaucratic hurdles that have followed in the wake of *Roe*'s repeal scheme unfairly restrict access for women with the least economic and social resources.

Furthermore, taxpayers may be more willing to pay for abortions under a scheme that restricts women's choices to those that are morally acceptable to the majority. And given the unwillingness of the courts to strike down laws barring public spending on abortion, taxpayer or voter support will be necessary to bring back abortion funding. To develop voter support for funding, reproductive rights advocates should consider Kristin Luker's advice to be mindful of public support for abortions women "need" but not for abortions that women merely "want."[85] Luker's comment suggests that poor, young, and geographically isolated women may have fared even better had the Court adopted the regulatory scheme proposed in 1967 by the AMA (based on a model law proposed by the American Legal Institute), which permitted only therapeutic abortions at each stage of pregnancy. Therapeutic abortions are abortions women need, though the public's conception of "therapeutic" may be somewhat narrow. Under an AMA-type scheme, for instance, it may be difficult for women to get abortions in the first trimester for socioeconomic hardships. In *Doe v. Bolton*, a case the justices were considering at the same time as *Roe*, a woman in Georgia requested an abortion on serious socioeconomic grounds and was turned down by a hospital committee. This case led many repeal advocates to reject reform schemes, such as the AMA proposal, which the Georgia law being challenged had incorporated.[86] Because it is likely to be difficult to get state legislatures to permit some abortions on socioeconomic grounds in reforming their laws, the ABA regulatory scheme, which would have required states to have some period for unrestricted abortions (roughly the first trimester), offers a compromise between reform and repeal schemes. This compromise may be capable of winning broad public support and, if so, would give women ample access to abortion if the funding restrictions and other bureaucratic obstacles now in place were removed.

Like Rhoden, Ronald Dworkin defends the viability cutoff for un-restricted abortion, although he recognizes that viability was not the only way the Court could have designated an upper limit for abortion on demand compatible with the right to privacy. He then writes: "But though a somewhat different scheme from the one Blackmun designed might have been acceptable . . . .[s]o important a decision should not be overruled . . . unless it was clearly wrong, and his decision was certainly not clearly wrong."[87] Dworkin argues that the viability time-frame, though not necessary, is appropriate for three reasons:

> First, at about the time of fetal viability but not much before, the brain may have developed sufficiently so that a primitive form of fetal sentience is possible. A fetus might then sensibly be said to have interests of its own. . . . Second, before the moment of fetal viability arrives, a pregnant woman has usually had ample opportunity to reflect upon and decide whether she believes it best and right to continue her pregnancy or to terminate it.[88]

Dworkin's third reason is that, after viability, the fetus is sufficiently developed such that to abort at that time without medical reasons would demonstrate a failure to treat the taking of human life in a seri-ous and responsible way.

Dworkin's combined reasons for defending viability are inade-quate. First, although viability may coincide with the onset of sen-tience, the criteria for sentience are highly disputable, and sentience and viability would diverge if sentience were thought to occur earlier. Moreover, even if viability could serve as a proxy for sentience, why not just stipulate the onset of sentience as the cutoff? Second, although a viability cutoff may provide women ample time to arrange an abor-tion, Dworkin hasn't shown that a period shorter than six months would be inadequate. Third, Dworkin fails to show that elective abor-tions at, say, five months demonstrate a sufficiently serious and respon-sible attitude toward the taking of human life.

Dworkin's claim that at the onset of sentience "a fetus might be said to have interests of its own" seems irrelevant to Dworkin's analy-sis of the legal and political issues at stake in the abortion debate. For Dworkin has argued that what justifies the government's regulation of abortion is not its duty to protect the fetus's interests or rights, for the fetus is not a person and thus does not have legal rights. Instead, what justifies the government's regulation of abortion is its responsibility for upholding fundamental social values, especially the intrinsic value of human life. Although a society may be divided about the moral and legal rights of human fetuses, belief in the sanctity of human life is a core social value and not subject to genuine dispute, according to Dworkin. Citizens may dispute the conditions or traits that make human life intrinsically valuable, but their differences about this, according to Dworkin, lead to different notions about how best to respect the sanctity of human life, which remains a core social value. Therefore, should the government restrict abortion, it should do so for the widely recognized purpose of upholding the value of human life, and in a way that recognizes that there are different ways to respect the value of human life, and not for the sake of protecting a set of interests that are widely contested. Some abortions, such as late nontherapeutic abortions, are inconsistent with any reasonable understanding of the principle that human life has inherent worth, and thus the government may restrict such abortions.

Dworkin claims that "at the point of fetal viability, the state may claim a legitimate interest that is independent of its interest in enforcing its conception of the sanctity of life."[89] At this point the state may restrict abortion to protect the fetus's interests, as long as it does so in a way that respects the rights of legal persons. However, when the state restricts abortion to protect the viable or sentient fetus's interests, it is enforcing not a fundamental social value but a theory of human development. And, unlike belief in the sanctity of human life, Dworkin's theory of human development is not widely shared nor a core social value. Some people believe that the fetus is endowed with a soul and has interests from the moment of conception. Others believe the fetus has interests only when it can form a concept of itself as a separate being (probably after birth). Dworkin contends that it has interests when it becomes sentient, presumably because then it has an interest in avoiding suffering, but he offers no sustained defense of this. Nevertheless, he would allow the state to enforce a sentience conception of fetal development on a public that is divided on this issue, often on religious grounds. His position that the state has a legitimate interest in protecting the viable fetus, because it is sentient, is inconsistent with his claim that: "A state may not curtail liberty, in order to protect an intrinsic value . . . when the community is seriously divided about what respect for that value requires, and when people's opinions about the nature of that value reflect essentially religious convictions that are fundamental to moral personality."[90] In the United States, citizens are divided over when the fetus has interests to protect, and their different views on this question reflect different religious convictions.[91] Dworkin, Newman, and Blackmun all agree that the state should not enforce a particular theory of when a human life begins, such as by stipulating that the fetus is a person, but they seem to approve the state's enforcement of a particular theory of proto-personhood on the basis of scientific, and therefore presumably neutral, criteria such as "sentience" or "viability." But endorsing a theory of when a proto-human life begins is no better than endorsing a theory of when a human life begins.

Dworkin's third reason for the appropriateness of viability is more compatible with his general analysis that, when the state regulates abortion, it is fulfilling its responsibility to uphold a fundamental social value. Although the state may not impose a particular way of respecting the sanctity of human life, it can proscribe actions that reflect indifference to this principle without violating our privacy or freedom of conscience. He argues that allowing states to prohibit nontherapeutic abortions at viability only prohibits actions that show indifference to a widely shared principle, not actions that reflect different understandings of this principle. Abortions after viability insult the principle that human life is inherently valuable because, when a fetus has made substantial progress toward infanthood, a significant natural and creative investment has been made in its life, according to Dworkin. The destruction of a such a fetus without medical cause would be extremely wasteful of this investment. Therefore, the woman who waits until late pregnancy to arrange an elective abortion shows indifference to the idea that human life is sacred and not simply a different understanding of what gives human life its intrinsic value.[92] But this argument only shows that we should restrict abortion at some point in late pregnancy, not necessarily at viability, which only happens now to coincide with late pregnancy. Moreover, stipulating viability as the cutoff for elective abortions may not be the most rational way for the state to proscribe actions that undermine the idea that human life has intrinsic value. If the natural and creative investment in the fetus increases gradually throughout pregnancy (and makes no significant jump at viability), then the earlier a woman arranges for an abortion, the less her abortion is wasteful of human life. Thus it would be better to have policies that encouraged women to arrange abortions as early as possible, well before the end of the second trimester, assuming it is feasible for them to do this. But having the cutoff for elective abortions at viability fails to encourage this.

Women often cannot arrange for early elective abortions because of the lack of funds to cover the costs, the increasing scarcity of providers, and the escalating bureaucratic and social hurdles imposed on them. Dworkin objects to both the withdrawal of government funds to pay for medically necessary abortions and the use of waiting periods, but maintaining viability as the cutoff for elective abortions offends the majority of citizens' beliefs about the moral gravity of a second trimester abortions and thus gives momentum to legislative proposals to limit abortions in ways he opposes.[93] An upper limit that is not sensitive to public opinion regarding when in a pregnancy an elective abortion shows indifference to the value of human life can fuel efforts to impede women who choose abortion. When these efforts are successful, then almost no amount of time—whether six or three months—is ample enough for some women to exercise their procreative autonomy. Although Marshall and Brennan sought to give women who might need it more time to arrange abortions, a woman's ability to arrange an abortion depends on the healthcare resources she can access and not only the amount of time she has. If we want to create the legislative will to provide these resources rather than take them away, we need to ensure that the timeframe for elective abortions respects widely shared values, such as the one Dworkin identifies.

Dworkin argues that the public is confused about the political and legal basis for restricting abortion, and that this, he writes,

> has poisoned the public controversy about abortion, and made it more confrontational and less open to argument and accommodation. The scalding rhetoric of the "pro-life" movement seems to presuppose the derivative claim that a fetus is from the moment of its conception a full moral person with rights and interests equal in importance to those of any other member of the moral community. But very few people—even those who belong to the most vehemently anti-abortion groups—actually believe that, whatever they say.[94]

Dworkin contends that what most people in fact believe is that human life is inherently valuable, although we disagree over what makes it valuable and therefore when the deliberate sacrifice of life is appropriate. Those who believe that human life reflects the work of a divine creator think differently about what gives human life value from those who believe that the unique capacity for consciousness and community with others is crucial. By attributing different views on abortion to our divergent reasons for holding the shared belief in the value of human life, rather than divergent views about fetal rights, Dworkin helps to render coherent the positions taken by both conservatives and liberals in this debate.

Although some lack of clear thinking about which values are at stake may have poisoned the abortion controversy, *Roe*'s regulatory scheme has probably had a greater toxic effect. Indeed the "pro-life" movement's "scalding rhetoric" and, especially, their scalding images of aborted, late-second-trimester fetuses, may signify their frustration with a regulatory environment that allows fetuses to be destroyed without medical or other serious reasons at this stage. This rhetoric need not presuppose that the fetus is a full person from the moment of conception. In a different regulatory environment, such rhetoric and images might prove less powerful, for example, if abortions—especially those most morally and visually troubling—were understood to result from legitimate need and not mere "choice." So, although the public may be confused about the basis of some governmental prohibitions, merely clarifying the interests the government may legitimately pursue will not make this controversy more responsive to argument and accommodation.

Dworkin hopes that by identifying the source of our disagreement over abortion as a spiritual one and then seeing that we share a belief in the sanctity of human life while disagreeing over how best to put this belief into practice, we might become more tolerant of those who disagree with us.[95] But his analytical separation of the different governmental interests involved in the abortion debate serves only to strengthen the privacy argument for liberal abortion laws, not to promote social tolerance. Dworkin argues that our abortion laws should be guided by legal and political traditions that respect the right of procreative autonomy, which means in part that states cannot arbitrarily expand the population of persons or interests in ways that would curtail the rights of indisputable persons. These traditions permit the state to proscribe actions that threaten foundational social values but not to protect private interests or rights not widely recognized. If he is right, then our regulations covering abortion should be guided by these traditions and not by the concept of viability, which serves as a poor proxy for them.

Viable Alternatives | Marshall's apparent understanding of "viability" as measure of a woman's access to medical and social resources, rather than a measure of general medical and technological proficiency, points the way to a different scheme for regulating abortion. For many women, access to medical care, or to economic resources that would enable them to assume parental responsibilities, is a function of the general social security provisions of their society. In some countries, the more the general social security net is regarded as inadequate, the more access women are given to abortion. For example, Mary Ann Glendon claims that in

> the West German and Spanish constitutional courts . . . there is the notion that what the pregnant woman can be required to sacrifice for the common value is related to what the social welfare state is ready and able to do to help with the burdens of childbirth and parenthood. For example, the Spanish court, reluctantly upholding the exception of a defective fetus, takes note of the hardship involved in raising a disabled child and the very limited degree of public assistance presently available in Spain. The statement intimates that the exception would need to be re-examined if and when the social state were able to alleviate the strain of raising disabled children.[96]

The reasoning of these courts recognizes that society must demand less of those who have less and conversely, that it can ask more of individuals when more social resources are made available to them. Instead of justifying abortion policies in terms of the right of individuals to be let alone, abortion policies are justified in terms of social interdependence and responsibility, and social expectations are enforced less when social support is absent.

When abortion policies are justified in terms of the right of individuals to be free of social or government interference, then the government's role is primarily negative in expanding women's reproductive choices. The more the government lets women alone, such as by extending the period for unrestricted abortion, the more choice women presumably have. However, *Roe* only restricts how states may use the criminal law to exert social control over the decision to abort, allowing state and federal officials to exert control by restricting access to medical care. Freedom from criminal prosecution expands the choices of affluent women and their doctors, but the reduction of public spending on abortion narrows the reproductive options of poor and young women. Because of this, the reproductive options of most women have not expanded following *Roe*. By contrast, poor women in European societies, which put less emphasis on individual autonomy and more on social responsibility, have greater access to first-trimester abortion, as well as to better health- and childcare for their dependents, and thus have more reproductive choices. So although the decision to abort is less protected from societal interference, when a woman's decision meets societal expectations, she has greater access to medical resources.

The rulings of the German Constitutional Court on abortion reflect the idea that the reasonableness of social expectations is partly a function of the resources society offers to help individuals meet these expectations. This court has ruled that abortion on demand is inconsistent with the value society places on each human life, but this court also recognizes the inappropriateness of coercing motherhood and nurture by threatening criminal sanctions. Accordingly, this court has encouraged state bureaucrats and legislators to develop public assistance programs that allow women to choose pregnancy over abortion without facing excessive personal hardship.[97] Women who can demonstrate that pregnancy poses serious hardships, even with economic support, have access to state-supported abortion services. Such policies show that the state values each life and will provide the resources necessary to enable women to nurture life. They also reflect the understanding that, in some cases, the state's help may not be enough to offset the hardships of pregnancy.

Unfortunately, in the United States, "pro-life" sentiments have not led to calls for better public assistance programs for poor families and single mothers. Instead they have led to calls to protect human embryos from destruction, including laboratory-produced embryos that might be used for research. Such strategies for protecting human lives are the result of extremely individualistic notions that see the government's role as limited to protecting individuals from assault but not from material impoverishment. When "pro-life" sentiments are mixed with a libertarian ethic of individual responsibility, the result is a society that imposes only a negative duty not to destroy human lives, while failing to recognize a positive duty to guarantee a minimum standard of living to the resulting parents and children. Such policies acknowledge little social responsibility for families that are vulnerable to poverty and its miserable effects, while adopting policies that result in the creation of greater numbers of vulnerable families. Furthermore, welfare policies that restrict women's access to abortion and contraception but penalize women for having children often give women little choice but to have abortions, if they can get them.[98] The welfare policies of the United States at present are set up to discourage both child-bearing and abortion. As Ruth Colker writes: "Until we, as a society, decide to protect life minimally by providing adequate prenatal care, postnatal care, childcare, and pregnancy leave, then it is hard to take seriously a government's claim that it is restricting abortion to protect its valuation of life. More likely, it is restricting abortion in order to display its disrespect for the lives of women."[99] A system that better reflects the value of human life is one that would show respect for women's childbearing, whether they be single or poor. Welfare policies that permit women to have the children they want, or obtain contraception and abortion to limit their own childbearing, show more respect for both children's and women's lives. Welfare policies such as these reflect the idea that what people are able to do is often a result of social cooperation and not just individual merit. By contrast, U.S. welfare policies demand personal responsibility without acknowledging society's responsibility for the material conditions that constrain people's lives.

Should the United States simply adopt the regulatory approach to abortion now in use in many liberal democratic social welfare states? Responding to Mary Ann Glendon, who proposes this, Ruth Colker writes: "I do not suggest it as the solution in the United States. That solution is only possible in a system with state-funded health care, including abortions."[100] Yet Glendon seems to suggest that we adopt not only the regulations but the larger security net as well. She writes:

> If we are to move from abortion on demand to reimposition of restrictions on abortions in certain situations, we should review the entire complex of laws that bear on maternity and child-raising, including but not limited to our welfare and child support laws. . . . The European experience leads one to wonder why pregnant women in the United States should be asked to make significant sacrifices . . . if absent fathers and the community as a whole are not asked to sacrifice too.[101]

The issue perhaps is this: How can we move toward an expanded social security net that allows women to choose motherhood or abortion, along with the reasonable regulations that a society providing this net would expect? The main difference between Glendon and Coker seems to be that Glendon prefers the more democratic route of the legislative process for achieving such policies, while Colker remains skeptical that majoritarian rule will benefit poor women and defends the importance of judicial review. In other words, Glendon wants the courts to let the legislatures resolve the issues of welfare and abortion access, whereas Colker thinks the courts should defend the abortion rights of women when the legislatures have done little to provide a security net.

Abortion rights activists in the United States have of course heavily relied on the judicial route to bring about change on abortion. But their main accomplishment, *Roe*, has remained unpopular. As Cass Sunstein points out, "judges are usually not effective in producing social reform."[102] Genuine social reform is more likely to come from grassroots political organizing than from on high. Abortion rights activists have also engaged in grassroots political organizing, but they have primarily organized around the ideas of "individual choice" and limiting the government's reach and have endorsed only the most minimal, libertarian regulatory schemes, not welfare reform. Indeed, the main difference between defenders and opponents of abortion rights in the United States is that the former stress individual choice while the latter stress individual responsibility. But these are just two sides of the same liberal individualist coin. To achieve policies that benefit the majority of women and not merely the affluent, we need to promote, both in the legislature and the courts, the ideas of social interdependence and responsibility and not merely the right to be let alone.

Feminist activists in the United States have generally not viewed abortion rights as contingent upon expanding social welfare programs, perhaps because it would make achieving the former seem almost hopeless. Instead, we have sought and won abortion policies that have resulted in both wide disparities of access and much social unrest. Poor women and women far from major urban centers often cannot obtain therapeutic abortions at eight weeks, while economically well-off women can obtain elective abortions at six months. And some require more expensive and riskier second-trimester abortions because of the obstacles they encounter when they try to arrange them earlier. In brief, it's a mistake to think that genuine procreative choice for most women can be achieved without universal healthcare, government-subsidized childcare programs, and income support and work security for poor families, as well as some period for abortion on demand. Speaking about the meaning of reproductive liberty for black and poor women, Dorothy Roberts writes that "their reproductive freedom . . . is limited not only by the denial of access to safe abortions, but also by the lack of resources necessary for a healthy pregnancy and parenting relationship. Their choices are limited not only by direct government interference in their decisions, but also by government's failure to facilitate them."[103] Roberts also criticizes the "pro-choice" movement for remaining "relatively complacent about the effective denial of access to abortions for poor women by the Supreme Court's decisions in the abortion-funding cases." Roberts claims that the movement's primarily motivation is "the threat to the reproductive rights of affluent women" and the fear that *Roe* might be overruled.[104] It may be that this movement has merely failed to recognize that securing six months of unrestricted abortion primarily benefits affluent women while it undermines public support for state spending on abortion services for poor women. Rickie Solinger has recently argued, the "pro-choice" conception of liberty underlying *Roe* has helped to transform both abortion and parenting into consumer choices—choices reserved for those who can afford them.[105] Poor women are viewed as entitled neither to the abortions they cannot afford nor to their children, since, instead of giving birth to children they cannot afford, they presumably could have had abortions. Whatever choice they make, they are now cast as irresponsible decision-makers. I have tried to show that the "pro-choice" conception of liberty reflects the ideas of repeal advocates, who ultimately influenced the *Roe* Court. The repeal conception of reproductive liberty has obscured for thirty years more reasonable regulatory schemes that could have avoided some of the backlash, whose effects have been felt most by poor women.

While *Roe* has not extended reproductive choice to the majority of women, it continues to be strongly challenged both politically and legally. Should it ever be successfully overturned, some states will outlaw all nontherapeutic abortions, moving us back to the pre-*Roe* era, when women could not obtain abortions for ordinary reasons, such as birth control failure or aspirations incompatible with childbearing, or when there were social and economic hardships, such as rape or a teen pregnancy. Some states' bans may include only narrow therapeutic exceptions, such as a threat to a woman's life or physical but not mental health. Yet one way to meet the attack on *Roe* is to acknowledge some of the problems with its regulatory scheme and to correct them, so that it need not be completely overruled. A shorter timeframe for abortions on demand, combined with broad therapeutic exceptions to abortion bans in the second trimester, may address many of the concerns the public has about abortion, bridging the gap between moderate abortion rights supporters and moderate "pro-life" proponents. In the next chapter, I argue that a scheme such as this is compatible with privacy reasoning. Yet a scheme such as this may violate a woman's right to equal protection, if the government does not make efforts to remove the obstacles that block a woman's access to an abortion permitted under its regulations.

One primary obstacle women face is the failure of private and public health insurance programs to pay for abortions. Some feminist lawyers are now challenging the discriminatory nature of insurance schemes that deny coverage for prescription drugs or devices used for contraception. Some argue that a woman must be able to limit the number of pregnancies she has in order to maintain her optimal health. Given that many forms of contraception are not fail-proof, early abortions are often necessary to enable a woman to control her fertility, and thus coverage for them can be defended on the same grounds. Yet abortion rights activists often try to avoid representing abortion as a kind of fertility control, even a control of last resort, because abortion is too controversial. Instead, women seeking abortions are often presented as seeking them for more desperate reasons than basic health maintenance. The mass media participates in the representation of abortion as a decision typically made for extraordinary reasons. Andrea Press and Elizabeth Cole write: "On television, middle-class or upper-class women seek abortion only in the most extreme cases: rape, incest, to save the mother's life, or if genetic testing reveals a severely deformed fetus." In 1972, viewer reactions to an episode of *Maude* in which Maude chose to have an abortion because she felt she was too old to raise a child so troubled sponsors that network TV now depicts women who are economically comfortable as choosing abortions only in extreme situations. Nevertheless, working-class women on TV are permitted to choose abortions in somewhat less extreme circumstances, but only as part of an admirable struggle to achieve economic security.[106] As abortion becomes a socially stigmatizing act, we imagine that only women in desperate social, medical, or economic circumstances would choose it. "Pro-choice" proponents often emphasize the desperate reasons for which women seek abortion and, in doing so, are contributing to the stigma placed on the act of abortion and the women who have them. However, if they had to defend only early elective abortion, they could emphasize the ordinary health reasons (spacing or limiting the number of pregnancies one attempts), as well as practical reasons (being too young or old, being single, and so on) for having an abortion and demand backup early abortion services for the same reasons women demand birth control. Defenses of the use of the "morning-after pill" and RU 486 often stress their use as backup birth control, and so could defenses of surgical abortion, if it was understood that its unrestricted use was limited to early pregnancy.

A somewhat narrower window for abortion on demand is not too invasive of privacy when women have insurance coverage for abortion services and when young women have access to information about contraception, sexuality, and pregnancy. With the availability of insurance coverage and convenient providers, most women can arrange abortions by twelve or fifteen weeks, though the exact upper limit is debatable. Many women seek abortions in order to delay childbearing or to better control the circumstances under which they carry through a pregnancy and raise a child. These abortions occur not because of an unusual health problem or because of socioeconomic desperateness but to serve ordinary individual ends. Having access to backup early abortions when other methods of contraception are inadequate, or simply not used rigorously, may be the optimal way, from a general health perspective, for women to avoid unwanted and potentially debilitating pregnancies.

The idea that many, and probably the majority of, women choose to abort for ordinary health, economic, or personal reasons provides a criterion for locating the upper limit for unrestricted abortions. Assuming that there are no special economic or social hurdles to obtaining an abortion, most abortions chosen for ordinary reasons can be arranged in the first third or half of pregnancy. Therefore, we can locate a point in the middle of this range to confer the right to abort without any questions asked, much as we locate a point in the middle of a range defined by a variety of factors to confer driving privileges. For women needing abortions in cases of serious or extreme hardship, the ordinary restrictions on abortions can be lifted. Such policies would encourage women to seek medical attention early in their pregnancies, which is generally a good thing, whether they elect to have abortions or not. And policies that create incentives for pregnant women who want abortions for ordinary reasons to arrange them early can be justified on the grounds of controlling healthcare costs and allocating scarce medical resources, as Blackmun suggested in defending his original scheme. Thus without resorting to the vague and irrelevant notion of "viability," or imposing an entirely arbitrary limit, we can locate a point for balancing individual choice with social (and not simply individual) responsibility.

Ad **Hoc Liberalism** | Moral and legal defenses of abortion typi-
cally appeal to some kind of liberty right: (1) the right to be free from
social coercion on matters of personal importance, such as procreation,
(2) the freedom to follow one's conscience on reasonably disputable
moral matters, (3) freedom from involuntary servitude, which encom-
passes the right to refuse to provide help—even critically needed assistance—to others, and (4) freedom from bodily invasion and injury.
The first defense assumes the fetus is not a person and thus that the
abortion decision should involve only one person. The second defense
assumes that the question of the fetus's personhood is irresolvable.
Given these assumptions, if the category of moral (or legal) persons
was enlarged to include fetuses, the first two defenses would be substantially weakened. However, the third and fourth defenses would
not be weakened, and some versions of the fourth defense would even
be strengthened if fetuses were regarded as full moral or legal persons. Nevertheless, the liberty rights asserted by the third and fourth
defenses admit of numerous exceptions; for example, parents may
not refuse to provide critically needed help to their children, and a
person's body may, in some circumstances, be invaded in order to
collect criminal evidence or to perform unwanted life-saving ther-
apy. In order to argue against those who allege that pregnancy falls
under one of the permissible exceptions to the third or fourth liberty
guarantees, some legal scholars bolster their liberty defense with
an appeal to equal protection. They argue that the pregnancy exception must be consistent with the exceptions made, or not made,
in comparable kinds of situations and for comparable kinds of actors,
or else the government will be treating those vulnerable to pregnancy
unequally, and that such unequal treatment constitutes invidious sex
discrimination.

In this chapter, I am not going to try to decide which of these abortion defenses has the greatest merit, either as a moral or constitutional argument. Like Anita Allen, I take an "additive approach" and recognize that each of these arguments helps to justify liberal abortion policies.[1] However, none of these arguments for abortion rights resolves the question of how broad these rights should be, so I will explore in more detail some reasonable ways to answer this question. Because these arguments are designed to expose the wrongness of governmental prohibitions on abortion, each defense must be supplemented with other considerations to rationalize the government's partial prohibition of abortion. In other words, liberal defenses of abortion typically yield arguments of the form: because a person should be free from X, Y, or Z, a woman should be free to abort her pregnancy. The conclusions of these arguments do not morally distinguish abortions performed early in a pregnancy from those performed late in a pregnancy, nor do they distinguish those performed for health, eugenic, or socioeconomic reasons from those performed without such justifications.

To avoid formulating conclusions and policies that ignore these distinctions and treat all abortions alike, contemporary liberal legal theorists enlist the concept of fetal "viability," which signifies the point in the fetus's development when it has some chance of extrauterine survival. In the nineteenth century, legal theorists often employed the concept of "quickening" to mark the point when abortions could be prohibited. In 1973, the Supreme Court selected "viability" over "quickening," because some justices believed that the former is grounded in science and medicine rather than religion. Like "quickening" the concept of "viability" enables the government to enforce a moderate "pro-life" view, in which abortions are permitted only until a particular point of fetal development is reached. By marking a discrete moment when a fetus qualifies for state protection, "viability" makes it possible to grant women a virtually unlimited right "to choose" for six months and then grant fetuses a qualified right "to life" for three months. According to Mark Tushnet, Justice Brennan "thought it would be helpful to abandon the word *viability*. Using that word suggested that the focus was on the state's interest in protecting the fetus, whereas the entire analysis otherwise focused on the woman's interests and the state's interest in protecting *her* health and safety."[2] Tushnet notes, however, that Brennan accepted "viability" as a criterion for demarcating a third phase of pregnancy, in which the state may regulate to protect potential life. As I argued in chapter 1, there is probably no longer any medical justification for regulating abortion to protect a woman's health, given that the procedures which can be used today, even in late pregnancy, are no more dangerous than childbirth. And the procedures available today render viability medically irrelevant, as there is little risk of live birth with D & E or D & X, and even with some induced deliveries. Nevertheless, there are interests at stake other than those of women or fetuses, such as society's interest in proscribing actions that contradict all reasonable ways of respecting the inherent value of human life and the public's interest in an efficient and fair distribution of medical resources. These interests justify some curtailment of privacy without assigning fetuses a quasi right to life.

In this chapter, I will explore the standard liberal defenses of abortion in order to see if they yield better, or simply less ad hoc, ways to justify limits on the right to abort. Articulating principled and satisfactory ways to limit the legal right to abort is important if we want to address legislative efforts that impose arbitrary and discriminatory limits on the right granted by the *Roe* Court.[3] I argued in chapter 1 that bureaucratic obstacles to legal abortion are sustained, in part, by the public's disapproval of abortion "on demand" in the second trimester rather than by lack of support for legal abortion. Permitting women to abort, in nontherapeutic cases, relatively mature fetuses exacerbates the abortion controversy and pushes each side to extreme positions. Yet providing a six-month upper limit for nontherapeutic abortions is neither necessary to ensure that women are able to avoid compulsory pregnancy nor good public policy, when we take into consideration the advantages of early abortions (in nontherapeutic cases). The purpose of this chapter is to investigate whether the standard arguments that support legal abortion should be understood to justify a right to unrestricted abortion up to six months of gestation. I will contend that the second and third defenses mentioned earlier, which I regard as the least problematic of the standard arguments, rest on principles that yield a right to abort more limited in scope than the right guaranteed in *Roe*. Furthermore, although the establishment of a narrower window for unrestricted abortion will not appease all opponents of legal abortion, it can promote the formation of democratic majorities supporting abortion rights. Forging such legislative majorities is necessary both to vote down discriminatory restrictions on abortion rights and to approve public spending on healthcare that includes legal abortion services.

Decisional Privacy | Defenses (1) and (2) mentioned earlier invoke the political notion of privacy. It is centrally important to our understanding of what it means to live in a free society that individuals be granted the sole authority to decide whom or if they will marry, when and how many children they will bear, the role of sex in their intimate relationships, and what if any religion to practice for themselves and their children. There are other candidates for this list, but the second and third items are the most relevant for the issue of abortion. They acknowledge the right of the individual to decide whether to bear children and whether to participate in sexual acts not aimed at procreation. The privacy defense of abortion essentially asserts that the government may not, without a compelling reason, compromise an individual's decisional authority over these matters and that prohibiting abortion would unreasonably infringe her authority.

Interestingly, some abortion opponents argue that an individual's decisional authority over sex and childbearing is compromised when the government permits abortion. These opponents argue that, in tolerating abortion, a society both gives its approval to nonprocreational sex and undermines the need for sexual abstinence in order to delay childbearing. In other words, by permitting abortion, a society gives preference to secular or atheistic understandings of sex and procreation—understandings that separate sex and procreation. In this way, by permitting abortion, the government interferes with an individual's right to decide the purpose of sex and what religion they or their children will practice, given that many religions take a negative view of nonprocreational sex.

Cass Sunstein regards the privacy defense of abortion as open to this objection. He points out that both conservatives and liberals on abortion assume a sphere of life in which relationships are ordered by natural forces, and both want to restrict the government's involvement in this sphere. For conservatives, the government's toleration of abortion unnaturally separates sexuality from reproduction, whereas for liberals, the government's prohibition of abortion unnaturally connects them.[4] Secular liberals typically hold that the sex drive serves purposes other than reproduction, whereas religious conservatives typically hold that sex and reproduction are connected by nature or God. Because views about the naturalness of nonreproductive sexuality reflect religiously based disagreements, Sunstein argues that the government should avoid taking sides on this issue. Instead, Sunstein prefers equality based defenses of abortion rights, which focus on eliminating invidious forms of discrimination. Sunstein holds that it falls within the government's legitimate authority to oppose sex discrimination, whereas it falls outside the government's authority to show a preference for secular understandings of human sexuality. However, the government's opposition to sex discrimination may be open to the same objection as the government's toleration of abortion. For conservatives can argue that, in opposing sex discrimination, the government is taking sides on the meaning of gender difference and the proper roles of men and women. That is, governmental restrictions on sex discrimination give preference to secular understandings of gender difference over traditional religious interpretations that assign distinct roles to each sex. In short, defenses of abortion that rest on the government's duty to eliminate sex discrimination are equally open to the objection that the government is illegitimately compromising its citizens' decisional autonomy. Defenders of equality approaches to abortion rights, like Sunstein, need to explain why the government should take sides on the meaning of gender difference but not the purpose of sexuality.

Because both privacy and equality based defenses of abortion are open to the objection that the government is establishing secular rationality in a way that interferes with the freedom to practice one's religion, it would be good to meet this objection head on. That is, we should question whether the government's toleration of abortion, or opposition to sex discrimination, gives preference to secular views of sexuality and gender difference in a way that compromises citizens' autonomy in important areas of life. One might argue that decisional autonomy requires that individuals are able to express divergent preferences and views as they pursue their own happiness and well-being. A government that prohibits abortion limits individual autonomy to a greater degree with respect to sex and procreation than one that permits it. For under the permissive government, individuals are able to a significant extent to live in accordance with their religiously based views of procreation, whereas the government that prohibits abortion imposes a religiously based conception of procreation on everyone. This defense of privacy based reasoning should also apply to equality based reasoning. Tolerating, rather than prohibiting, sex discrimination in public institutions denies individuals the freedom to express divergent beliefs about the meaning of gender difference in their public and private lives. Conversely, prohibiting sex discrimination in the public distribution of rights and opportunities does not unreasonably undermine citizens' autonomy by giving preference to secular understandings of gender difference. This is because citizens are still able to a significant extent to live in accordance with their religiously based views of gender difference. In short, under a government that permits abortion and forbids sex discrimination, individuals are reasonably free to avoid abortions and conform to traditional sex roles, whereas under a government that forbids abortion and tolerates sex discrimination, individuals are not reasonably free to have abortions or assume social roles not traditional to their sex. Therefore, permitting abortions and prohibiting sex discrimination better protects citizens' decisional autonomy over sex, procreation, and gender difference than the opposite policies.

Anita Allen defends privacy as a basis for abortion rights against arguments promoting equality based ones. Allen regards an individual's control over her reproductive capacities as a necessary component of personal freedom and not merely a means to social equality. Maintaining control over one's reproductive capacities grants to the individual the authority to decide whether to assume parental or caretaking responsibilities. When society imposes such duties on women, according to Allen, it limits "their opportunities for individual forms of privacy and independently chosen personal association."[5] Allen argues that "meaningful opportunities for personal privacy consist of quality time and space for one's self,"[6] something that caretakers give up to a large degree. Laws that interfere with a woman's ability to control her reproductive capacities deprive women of the time and space they have to attend to their own needs and force them into involuntary associations that involve attending to the needs of others. This loss of control not only prevents women from exercising their citizenship rights on an equal basis with men but also deprives them of forms of personal freedom that should be integral to a free society. Thus equality and privacy are both reasons for supporting abortion rights, but they are distinct reasons. A society in which the inability to control one's reproductive capacities burdened men and women equally with caretaking responsibilities and unchosen personal associations would be one in which women would be more equal. But it would be one in which people lacked to a significant degree the ability to control their personal and interpersonal destinies. For this reason, Allen argues it is important to defend the value of privacy, or a zone of life outside of legitimate social concern, and to defend abortion rights as part of privacy.

Allen also defends privacy based reasoning against those who allege that *Roe*'s privacy rationale is responsible for the withdrawal of public funding for abortion. Allen argues that the legal recognition of the right to be left alone is not inconsistent with government programs that help poor women obtain abortions. She reiterates a point made by others, that privacy recognizes not only the government's negative duty not to interfere but its positive obligation to ensure that a person's decisions about childbearing are free and informed. Fulfilling this positive obligation requires government spending on programs that give women access to information and reproductive healthcare services. Allen also points out the weaknesses of equal treatment approaches in generating positive obligations to help the poor. She writes:

> The logic of equal protection in American constitutional law has not always demanded that the poor be given the resources needed to make them the substantive equals of other citizens. Equality is open in our jurisprudence to quite thin "equal opportunity" rather than "equality of results" interpretations. The Court could have acknowledged the goal of abolishing discriminatory abortion laws, while ruling that the Constitution's Equal Protection Clause does not require government abortion subsidies.[7]

Yet Allen's criticism of legal reasoning about equality applies equally well to jurisprudence on privacy. The protection of decisional privacy has not typically been understood to mean that the poor be given the resources needed to ensure that their decisions are freely made. As Jeremy Waldron points out, the homeless often have no place where they can legally, let alone freely, choose to sleep or go to the bathroom, and yet the homeless have won few government subsidies.[8] That is, neither the extreme inability of homeless persons to exercise decisional authority over their bodily needs nor their extreme lack of physical privacy have been understood by the courts to require a level of government support that would end homelessness. Similarly, although the inaccessibility of abortion services may render a woman's procreative choices considerably less free, the courts are not likely for this reason to require that the government subsidize the costs of abortions.

I have argued that the privacy rationale alone was not responsible for the withdrawal of public funds. Instead, it was the inability of the justices to square the privacy rationale with a regulatory scheme that the public would find acceptable. Unfortunately, Blackmun, Marshall, Powell, and others became convinced that a six-month window for nontherapeutic abortion was more compatible than a three-month window with the privacy justification they articulated. Requiring states to permit abortion for any reason, even in the second trimester, led legislators, with the approval of their constituents, to devise alternative ways to restrict access to abortion. Had the Court adopted a regulatory scheme more compatible with public sentiments, there would have been less legislative momentum for imposing additional constraints. Although *Roe's* appeal to a fundamental right of privacy has been weakened, it has been weakened in ways that permit the greater bureaucratic regulation of abortion, through funding restrictions and mandatory patient counseling, parental notification or approval, and physician reporting requirements. Unfortunately, regulating access to abortion in these ways disproportionately affects young and poor women. The viability timeframe for nontherapeutic abortion has not been revised, although revising it would be a better way to impose reasonable restrictions on abortion. Of course, revising the viability timeframe now and allowing states to place therapeutic requirements on second-trimester abortions will not in itself remove the bureaucratic obstacles that have been erected. However, having a scheme that is compatible with public sentiments on abortion could defuse the legislative momentum to add further restrictions, and it would represent a first step toward building the legislative majorities necessary to remove existing bureaucratic barriers.[9]

Even though there may be strategic grounds for narrowing the time span for abortion "on demand," we need to explore further whether the privacy rationale for abortion rights is conceptually compatible with a cutoff earlier than six months. In the last chapter, I argued that the privacy defense offered by Ronald Dworkin supports an earlier cutoff for nontherapeutic abortion, contrary to his own defense of the viability criterion. Dworkin grounds the right to procreative autonomy on the premise that the government cannot limit freedom when there are religiously based, deep disagreements regarding the interest served by curtailing freedom. Yet this reasoning concedes the right of the government to curtail freedom when the members of a society generally recognize and agree on the overriding importance of the interest served. Dworkin points out that U.S. citizens are divided over when a fetus may claim rights equal to a legal person, but they generally adhere to the idea that human life is intrinsically valuable. Although some abortions are consistent with this idea, some abortions contradict all reasonable interpretations of it.

It is not wrong to destroy an entity of intrinsic value, if destroying it would preserve something of greater intrinsic worth or if the attributes that give the entity intrinsic value are not significantly developed or capable of development. An abortion performed to preserve something of greater inherent value (such as a woman's life, health, or socioeconomic security), and/or involving a fetus whose human traits are undeveloped, is consistent with the idea that human life has intrinsic value. By contrast, an abortion that is not necessary to preserve a woman's life, health, or socioeconomic security, and that destroys a basically healthy fetus whose human attributes are significantly developed, is not consistent with this principle. Dworkin has argued that the government may curtail freedom not to protect a fetus's rights, which are in dispute, but to advance the state's interest in promoting respect for the intrinsic value of human life. If some abortions are inconsistent with all reasonable interpretations of the idea that human life is intrinsically valuable, then the government may proscribe these abortions. Thus the government may proscribe abortions that are not necessary to preserve something of greater value and that destroy something possessing the attributes that give entities intrinsic value.

Admittedly, it is difficult to say when the characteristics that make human life inherently valuable are evident in the fetus and when an abortion is necessary to preserve a woman's life, health, or socioeconomic security. It may be fairly clear that a seven-week embryo or a fetus that develops without a brain do not possess these characteristics, or that an abortion is necessary to preserve the health and socioeconomic security of a fourteen-year-old, a rape victim, or a cancer patient. But there are likely to be many borderline cases. Perhaps deciding these cases will prove as difficult as deciding when the fetus has interests deserving state protection. I argued in the last chapter that "viability" is a vague concept, subject to changing definitions as medical knowledge and technology advances. Moreover, practitioners can disagree over when a fetus's chances of survival are high enough and what is meant by "survival" or by *Roe*'s phrase "capability of meaningful life outside the mother's womb." Because of this, a line drawn at viability is no brighter than a line drawn at abortions contradicting the widely shared belief in the sanctity of life.

Identifying abortions that contradict all reasonable interpretations of a widely shared principle does not give us a bright line at a particular moment of pregnancy but only a limit contingent upon circumstances. If the waste of human life involved in an abortion increases as a pregnancy advances, then the hardships justifying this waste must be increasingly serious at each subsequent stage of pregnancy. For example, though the socioeconomic security of the pregnant woman may be something to consider, say, before twenty weeks, it may not be a justifying circumstance after that point. I would think that threats to the life or long-term physical health of the pregnant woman should be justifying circumstances at all stages of pregnancy, given the greater intrinsic worth of the woman's life (i.e., her relatively greater possession of traits that give human life value). Alternatively, denying a woman the modest health advantages of, for example, a D & X at twenty-three weeks over a full-term caesarean delivery in a healthy pregnancy may not be a sufficient hardship to justify destroying a fetus at this stage of development. Again, alternatively, the fetus's relative lack of traits that give human life value in the first ten or so weeks of pregnancy may render almost any reason a woman has for an abortion sufficient, thus justifying some period of abortion simply "on demand." In sum, a regulatory scheme that allows for up to ten or twelve weeks of unrestricted abortion and abortions for severe socioeconomic hardship and broad health reasons (including mental health) for a period of up to perhaps twenty weeks and for a narrow set of health reasons after that, would be supported by Dworkin's privacy argument. Although I am sure this scheme could be improved, it shows that the privacy defense neither entails nor justifies the regulatory scheme imposed by *Roe*. Moreover, at least Dworkin's version of this defense is compatible with a scheme having a somewhat narrower window for nontherapeutic abortions, followed by various kinds of exemptions at subsequent stages of pregnancy.

Although the privacy defense is consistent with a more moderate regulatory scheme and is not incompatible with public funding of abortion, and although it does not take sides on the purpose of sex (as Sunstein maintains), privacy based reasoning is not the only avenue for defending abortion rights. In the following sections, I will explore alternative defenses of abortion in order to extrapolate additional principles for regulating abortion. I will try to show that the third defense of abortion I listed at the beginning of this chapter justifies a right to abort whose scope converges with the right supported by Dworkin's privacy defense.

The Equal Right to Deny Help | Donald Regan writes, "It is a deeply rooted principle of American law that an individual is ordinarily not required to volunteer aid to another individual who is in danger or in need of assistance. In brief, our law does not require people to be Good Samaritans."[10] Regan argues that by forbidding abortion and compelling a women to gestate and deliver a fetus, we compel her to be a good Samaritan. Regan acknowledges that, under some circumstances, a person is legally required to give assistance to others. For instance, when someone has a special relationship with another person— such as a parent with a child, an innkeeper with a guest, a ship captain with a passenger, and so on—and the latter person requires critical assistance while in the custody of the former, then the custodial person, or person in charge, has an obligation to provide help.[11] Similarly, when someone begins to offer aid, she may not in some cases withdraw assistance if doing so would leave the recipient worse off than that person would have otherwise been if the rescuer had not begun to assist.[12] Furthermore, a person whose actions harm or endanger others, even unintentionally, is obligated to act so as to minimize the harm or danger to others.[13]

Regan argues against those who compare a pregnant woman to a person in a special relationship with the needy person, the person who has begun to offer aid, or the person whose actions place others in danger. First, a woman with an unplanned pregnancy has not voluntarily entered a relationship with the fetus. Regan argues that the obligation to aid follows only when one has chosen the status or relationship on which the obligation is based. Second, although a pregnant woman has begun to offer aid to a fetus, again she has not necessarily offered her services voluntarily. Moreover, her withdrawal of support leaves the fetus no worse off than before she began to assist it, for its prospects of survival or getting help are no worse than before she began to help. Third, her conduct, which includes conceiving and partially gestating the fetus, does not harm or endanger the fetus because, again, the fetus is left in the same condition after an abortion (nonexistence) as before she conceived it. Thus, Regan concludes that none of these common exceptions that permit the state to compel aid from someone are appropriate in the case of pregnancy.

Regan bolsters the "right not to be a good Samaritan"[14] argument in the following way. Even if pregnancy fit one of these exceptions, by compelling a woman to gestate a fetus, we impose on her burdens that are more physically invasive and demanding than the rescue duties we impose on others when they fall under these exceptions.[15] Therefore, compelling a woman to gestate a fetus to fulfill her duty to aid violates her right to equal protection under the laws. Regan concedes that if states were to pass statutes that required citizens to perform difficult and demanding rescues, and if such statutes were not held unconstitutional (and Regan thinks some might not be), then in this legal context a woman's duty to rescue a fetus could be legally commanded by the state without violating her right to equal treatment.[16] But, because our current statutory context does not require most citizens to attempt physically demanding rescues, the government may not pass laws that impose such rescues only on a particular group. Were the current statutory context to change, this would alter the constitutionality of abortion prohibitions. Regan acknowledges that the military draft or laws that require citizens to participate in a defense of the nation or their communities already obligate citizens to perform physically risky rescues. Yet he argues that there is a crucial difference, in that "the woman is being required to aid a specific other individual (the fetus); the draftee is not. Rightly or wrongly, our tradition distinguishes between obligations to aid particular individuals and obligations to promote a more broadly based public interest."[17]

Regan anticipates the objection that the legal requirement to rescue fellow citizens does serve a broad public interest, in the same way that the legal requirement not to harm fellow citizens does. He writes:

I am protected by law against gratuitous physical assault, and that suggests that in some sense there must be a public interest in so protecting me. Still, the public interest involved is ultimately based on my private interest in physical integrity. Similarly, if the prohibition on abortion is justified on the ground that the fetus has a right to life (as it commonly is these days), then the ultimate public interest is in protecting the private interest of the fetus.[18]

However, Dworkin's privacy defense suggests that prohibitions on abortion can be justified not derivatively in terms of the fetus's private rights or interests but on the grounds that they further society's interest in upholding the inherent value of human life. If this defense is sound, then there is an identifiable public interest served by prohibiting some abortions, an interest that is not derived from another individual's interest. Therefore, prohibiting those abortions that cheapen the value of human life would serve society's interest in upholding an important value. Consequently, if the government may require physically risky and demanding service of citizens to promote an important public interest, then it may do so in some cases of pregnancy.

Cass Sunstein has argued that although others are required to perform difficult rescues to defend important social interests, such as men who are drafted into military service, this does not prove that women are not treated unequally when abortions are prohibited. Instead, both the male-only military draft and prohibitions on abortion enlist those with certain sex-linked bodily capacities into forms of service that reflect sex role stereotyping and thereby constitute invidious sex discrimination. He writes:

> From the standpoint of equal protection, the problem with restrictions on abortion is not merely that they impose on women's bodies but also that they do so in a way that is inextricably intertwined with the prescription, by the law and thus the state, of different roles for men and women, different roles that are part of a second-class citizenship for women. Far from undermining it, the fact that only men are drafted helps to confirm the claim that abortion laws represent a form of unacceptable selectivity. [19]

Although a military draft could be imposed on women, which would escape Sunstein's equal treatment objection, abortion prohibitions inevitably seem to compel pregnancy service only of women. If pregnancy service could be imposed on men, abortion restrictions would not then select only women for the performance of stereotypical female roles. But given that men are incapable of pregnancy service at the present time,[20] abortion prohibitions serve to legally segregate women into forms of service that reflect and perpetuate harmful sex-role stereotypes.

Regan argues that pregnancy service is unique in the physical demands it makes on women's bodies, whereas Sunstein stresses that our willingness to enlist women's bodies in fetal care originates from biased thinking. Suppose, though, that the government compelled men to perform service that similarly involved the physical care of children—care that, though less physically invasive of the caretaker, would nevertheless require men's physical labor.[21] For example, suppose men were legally required to provide physical care for their biological offspring for some period of time after birth. Such a policy might be justified by society's interest in the welfare of children, especially if it were widely believed that having fathers participate in primary childcare duties was critical to children's psychological development. In this context, the government's imposition of pregnancy duty on women would avoid segregating men and women into stereotypical roles. Men who were unwilling to provide some period of physical care duties would be subject to penalties comparable to those for women who have illegal abortions. The law might allow men who are unfit caretakers, or who are physically unable to provide this care, to arrange for substitute caretakers in some cases, just as it may allow women who are ill suited for pregnancy to obtain early abortions. In a legal context such as this, and one I find somewhat attractive, Sunstein's objection would be significantly less serious. One would have to object on the basis of the physical invasiveness of compulsory pregnancy as opposed to compulsory physical childcare. But this is a different sort of objection from Sunstein's stereotypical treatment objection, and one that could be met by highlighting the physical challenges involved in the care of small infants and children (sleep deprivation, propensity for back strain, stress, etc.).

Regan's and Sunstein's "equal right to refuse to help" arguments both emphasize that bans on abortion should not select women for forms of service that are not required of others. Regan adds another constraint:

> [A]ny inequality that flows from an unchosen and unalterable characteristic is likely to be specially resented. It also works against the idea, deeply rooted in our culture, that people ought to be masters of their own destinies, at least within the limits of legally acceptable behavior that apply to everyone. Since pregnancy happens only to women, and since no one has any choice about whether to be a woman, susceptibility to pregnancy (and to being in the position of wanting an abortion) is a nonchosen characteristic.[22]

Here Regan appeals to the idea that the law should not enable differences of biology to translate unnecessarily into social inequalities. The question is: Does the law do this if it bans some abortions, especially late abortions?

Regan addresses the issue of when the state should restrict access to abortion. Like Dworkin, Regan tries to show that his constitutional defense better justifies the regulatory scheme in *Roe* than the rationale used by the Court. He argues that the Court's privacy based reasoning does not explain why, once the government can invade a woman's privacy at viability for the sake of the fetus, it can only do so in a limited way. Specifically, according to Regan, "it is not clear why the state's compelling interest (as the Court describes it) in protecting the potential life of a fetus already capable of 'meaningful life outside the mother's womb' (in the Court's phrase) is outweighed even by the woman's life, much less by her health."[23] By contrast, characterizing abortion as a refusal to rescue makes it clear why the fetus's right is subordinated to the woman's, for a rescuer is not required to sacrifice her life or health. However, Regan's view may leave unexplained how a fetus can acquire a right to some protection in late pregnancy when continuing the pregnancy does not threaten the woman's life or health. Should a rescuer be expected to endure the physical demands of late pregnancy in order to help a fetus when doing so would not sacrifice her life or health?

Regan makes a small attempt to elaborate the circumstances under which a fetus acquires a right to a particular woman's help. First, he asks "whether [his] argument justifies *all* of the result [in *Roe*]. In particular, does it justify drawing a line at the end of the second trimester, after which abortion may be generally forbidden?"[24] He then answers this question as follows.

> I think the Court's line between the second and third trimester can be justified on the ground that the woman who allows her pregnancy to reach the third trimester without having an abortion (assumed to be permissible in the first two trimesters) has waived her right of non-involvement with the fetus. Surely by the end of the second trimester a woman has had knowledge of her pregnancy long enough to have had a reasonable time to think through the difficult issue of whether she wants an abortion. There is a genuine state interest in encouraging decision at the earliest reasonable opportunity, even if it is only the interest in avoiding the greater dismay of many members of the public at late abortions. Admittedly, the argument does not tell us precisely where the "waiver" line should be. But if we consider the possibilities for denial by the woman early in the pregnancy, the difficulty of the issue for many women, and, on the other hand, the desirability of some clear line so long as it is not too early, a line at the beginning of the third trimester seems a reasonable solution.[25]

In this passage, Regan echoes the concerns of others who have wrestled with the timeframe for unrestricted access. That six months is "long enough" echoes the concerns of Newman, and that women may deny their condition, echoes the concerns of Marshall. That the state has an interest in encouraging early decisions (e.g., the health of the woman and fetus, the medical resources needed for abortions at different stages, etc.) echoes the concerns of Blackmun. Interestingly, in identifying the state's interest as "avoiding the greater dismay of many members of the public at late abortions," Regan anticipates Dworkin's idea that some abortions insult widely shared and fundamental social values, such as the inherent value of human life. Regan adds another idea to these concerns, that by six months a woman "has waived her right of non-involvement with the fetus." In a footnote to this passage Regan adds: "Actually it seems to me that a reasonable American legislature could probably put the 'waiver' line *somewhat* earlier. But I cannot be sure of that without looking more carefully than I have at the mechanics of arranging abortions for women in various circumstances."[26]

In another footnote to this passage, Regan acknowledges that his suggestion that there is a public interest in encouraging early abortions is prima facie inconsistent with his view that abortion prohibitions do not serve a genuinely "public" interest. He then writes that "if there is sufficient public interest to support a requirement that the woman decide whether to have an abortion by a certain time, why may not the abortion be forbidden on the basis of the same interest? A full answer to this question would require an extensive discussion of constitutional 'waiver' theory. I shall not give a full answer."[27] There are two issues here. One is whether compelling pregnancy service advances a genuinely public interest. The other issue is when a pregnant woman's right to refuse to help should be waived in order to advance this interest.

Dworkin's argument that the state has a legitimate interest in prohibiting actions that degrade or disrespect the value of human life addresses the first issue. Moreover, as Blackmun's statements and the *Roe* scheme suggests, the additional medical risks of late abortions, as well as the higher expenditure of scarce medical resources they require, justify regulatory guidelines that are increasingly restrictive as a pregnancy progresses.[28] Furthermore, when late pregnancy abortion procedures risk unanticipated live births, there are public interests at stake, as Rhoden has argued. Contra Regan, then, full consideration of the public interest issue does not require "an extensive discussion of constitutional 'waiver' theory," although full consideration of when a pregnant woman's right of noninvolvement should be waived may require this.

Yet in his discussion of Samaritanism and the law, Regan already substantially addresses the general conditions under which a person's right to noninvolvement should be waived. If we apply these conditions to pregnancy, then we should ask the following question: Does the voluntary endurance of a pregnancy for three, four, or five months constitute entering a special relationship with someone, beginning a rescue, or creating a hazard that leaves someone worse off than she or he would otherwise have been? If so, then by enduring a pregnancy over some specified period of time, voluntarily or passively, a woman may waive her right to refuse to help when helping does not impose unreasonable costs on her. Regan has argued that, for the woman seeking an abortion, "her entire course conduct" does not make her a suitable candidate for compulsory service. His argument assumes though that the entire course of her conduct merely includes unintentionally conceiving and then intentionally aborting a pregnancy. An unintentional conception implies that a woman has not entered a relationship with or begun to aid the fetus voluntarily. And because the fetus did not exist prior to the entire course of her conduct, her actions do not leave someone worse off than before. However, if we include in the entire course of her conduct the endurance of the pregnancy for, say, three, four, or five months, when she could have obtained an abortion at two or three months, does she passively enter a relationship, and does she leave the fetus worse off than it would have been had she discontinued aid earlier?

A woman who genuinely has the opportunity to abort but delays her abortion for a month or more is perhaps allowing herself to enter a relationship with an entity that is increasingly acquiring human traits and capacities. Moreover, the entire course of her conduct may make the fetus worse off than it would have been had she not delayed, because it may subject the fetus to a worse death than it otherwise could have had. A woman who aborts later than she could have imposes death on a creature that is more developed and sentient. Furthermore, abortion in the second trimester typically involves death by dismemberment, craniotomy, or the injection of a chemical that causes cardiac arrest, whereas abortion in the first trimester involves a less physically violent killing and dying process. In early abortions, the removal of the fetus causes death, and removal does not require crushing or cutting apart a living thing. Thus, the kind of death imposed on an older fetus seems qualitatively worse than the kind of death imposed on a younger fetus, both because an older fetus is a more developed and sentient creature and because the safe abortion of a pregnancy involving an older fetus involves a high degree of physical violence to the fetus.[29]

Jeff McMahan writes that one of the principal reasons death is bad is that it deprives its victims of future goods.[30] Another principal reason is that the dying process can involve physical suffering, the loss of valuable physical and mental capacities, disfigurement, and the loss of dignity. The more these aspects are present in a dying process, the worse it is. A woman who delays her withdrawal of support thereby subjects the fetus to a death in which these aspects are present to a greater degree. This doesn't mean that she should not be permitted an abortion, but it does mean that it is reasonable for society to expect reasons justifying the delay and to expect increasingly serious reasons as the pregnancy advances.[31] In sum, a woman who delays an abortion for weeks and months may be a suitable candidate for compulsory service to a fetus, if the service required of her is not unreasonably demanding or costly. Such service could fulfill a duty to aid required of all similarly situated citizens, and the laws requiring pregnancy service in such circumstances would serve a variety of public interests.

Regan not only regards a pregnant woman as an unsuitable candidate for compulsory service, he argues that even if she were, the services required of a woman denied an abortion would be wrong to impose. Thus, although she may make the fetus somewhat worse off, as I have argued, burdening her with months of pregnancy may go beyond the level of help society can demand. Regan claims that:

> In addition to imposing burdens greater than any of the recognized exceptions to the bad-Samaritan principle (except possibly the parenthood exception), anti-abortion laws also impose burdens of a *kind* that is especially suspect in our law. We are traditionally very dubious about practices which involve direct invasions of the body or the imposition of physical pain or extreme physical discomfort.[32]

Regan offers examples of what he calls "judicial squeamishness about physical invasion, pain, and discomfort."[33] He considers various court rulings pertaining to corporal punishment, to invasive and painful therapies performed on incarcerated individuals, and to mandatory donations of bodily substances, such as bone marrow. There are good reasons to oppose these practices. One reason is that their aims and potential benefits are quite questionable. Another is they potentially involve exploiting people to serve ends not necessarily of benefit to the person exploited. Yet when such actions serve worthy goals and under conditions that are not exploitative, such as a minor surgery that saves the patient's own life or a mandatory blood donation system to ensure an adequate blood supply for all, I'm not convinced the courts should be so "squeamish." Moreover, if bodily impositions are inherently suspect and not merely suspect when the goals are questionable or exploitative, shouldn't the courts consider the bodily impositions that a late abortion involves for a fetus—possibly dismemberment or craniotomy? I agree with Regan that the question of what level of service the state should compel from a suitable candidate is a difficult one, although not primarily because it involves bodily impositions. Indeed, the most severe burdens of compulsory pregnancy may be emotional ones, if a woman faces giving a child up for adoption, or perhaps economic ones if she decides to keep it.

Regan's reluctance to permit the state to command pregnancy duty may derive from his assumption that the right not to be a good Samaritan entails the right to be a bad Samaritan. By contrast, Judith Thomson, whose Samaritan analogy influenced Regan's account, does not defend a woman's right to be a bad Samaritan. Instead, she defends a pregnant woman's right to be no more than a minimally decent Samaritan. Thomson writes: "I should think, myself, that Minimally Decent Samaritan laws would be one thing, Good Samaritan laws quite another, and in fact highly improper."[34] Thomson offers some hints about the level of help she would require of a minimally decent Samaritan by describing circumstances in which an abortion would meet or fall below the minimum standard of decency.

> There may well be cases in which carrying the child to term requires only Minimally Decent Samaritanism of the mother, and this is a standard we must not fall below. . . . [A] sick and desperately frightened fourteen-year-old schoolgirl, pregnant due to rape, may *of course* choose abortion, and that any law which rules this out is an insane law. . . . [I]n other cases resort to abortion is even positively indecent. It would be indecent in the woman to request an abortion, and indecent in a doctor to perform it, if she is in her seventh month, and wants the abortion just to avoid the nuisance of postponing a trip abroad.[35]

Here Thomson suggests that two further months of pregnancy duty, when a woman is seven months pregnant, does not exceed the level of service a society can expect.

Unfortunately, Thomson's examples for distinguishing the minimally decent from the good Samaritan only give us a rough idea of when having an abortion would place a woman below the minimally decent standard. Meredith Michaels has argued that Thomson assumes the existence of shared moral standards for setting minimal Samaritan obligations and that because there are no widely held standards her defense of abortion falls apart.[36] Michaels is probably right that there are no universally held moral standards regarding the minimally decent thing to do in helping others. But there may be standards of moral responsibility that are widely enough held to justify constraints on some abortions and not others. Consider, for example, Thomson's well-known analogy comparing an unplanned pregnancy with a kind of abduction. In this analogy, a person finds that a famous, but sick, violinist has been hooked up to her circulatory system overnight, and then is told that the violinist will die if he is unplugged before nine months. I think this analogy has been influential because it taps into widely shared beliefs about what we owe to others and what we don't. This is not to say that this example would convince everyone that some abortions are compatible with decency, for some people expect greater sacrifices from others, especially from women whose bodies, some claim, are intended by God or nature for childbearing. But I would guess that Thomson's violinist analogy is powerful for the majority of U.S. citizens. Similarly, Thomson's example of the woman who requests a late abortion in order to avoid postponing a trip is likely to smack most Americans as unacceptably selfish. I am not suggesting that the reactions of the majority to these examples are necessarily right, and perhaps we need to educate ourselves in ways that would change our responses to these cases. But our reactions to these cases may indicate that there is sufficient agreement regarding the level of help we owe to others to justify minimally decent Samaritan laws. Such laws should impose comparable burdens on all citizens, or they would discriminate unfairly against people vulnerable to pregnancy.

Francis Kamm introduces the idea of the "good enough parent," which may help define the minimal Samaritan duties that the state may impose on a pregnant woman. She employs the notion of the "good enough parent" to suggest that the state cannot require people to be ideal parents, only minimally satisfactory parents.[37] For example, a woman who refuses to give up smoking while pregnant may meet minimum standards for parenting. Kamm argues that even though the child would be better off if the woman quit smoking, the child's interest in good health does not automatically create an obligation for a particular kind or level of support. The fetus inhabiting the body of a smoker may have reduced health, but the fetus in this situation is merely denied a benefit that it could gain only by a more imposing use of its biological mother's body. Kamm claims that the fetus is not necessarily entitled to a more imposing use of the woman's body—one that, for example, required her to overcome her cigarette habit and addiction. Because the fetus is a guest in the woman's body and not a co-occupant or owner, it is therefore only entitled to a level of use above a set minimum that the woman is willing to give. In short, a pregnant woman not seeking an abortion should be held responsible for supporting the fetus in a way that, in normal circumstances, will allow it to be born reasonably healthy, but the state should not compel a woman to provide her fetus a level of support likely to guarantee superior health at birth. Of course, there is room for disagreement regarding the meaning of "reasonably healthy" (e.g., the child residing in the body of a cocaine addict probably fails to meet this standard, but does the child of a moderate alcohol drinker?), and we may feel that good parents should provide levels of support above the minimum. Yet the state exceeds its authority when it compels parents to be ideally good and not simply good enough. Compelling parents to meet set minimum standards of parental care may involve a significant amount of social coercion, and it should be noted that Kamm's arguments do not imply that the state should use punitive means to accomplish this. Her arguments are compatible with the state's use of educational campaigns and health programs to help people overcome addiction or other problems that prevent them from providing minimally adequate care.

Although Kamm introduces the "good enough parent" notion, she does not extend this idea to the "good enough pregnant person" who seeks an abortion. That is, her general defense of the right to abort elaborates the right-to-be-a-bad-Samaritan strategy and not Thomson's right to be only a minimally decent Samaritan. Kamm argues that a woman who conceives and aborts a fetus has not made it worse off relative to the prospects it had before she conceived it. For a short life (at least one above a minimum quality) is not worse than no life. Even though the fetus would be better off with the woman's continued support, it is not entitled to her support, or to the benefits it could only obtain and retain with her support. Moreover, a woman is entitled to withdraw support, even if that involves killing the fetus, if there is no way at reasonable cost to the woman to discontinue her support without killing the fetus. Kamm writes: "This principle explains why, though the person killed is harmed relative to his improved condition in your body, he is not wronged in being harmed."[38] That is, although abortion involves a life-depriving act, the fetus could not have had its life without the woman's support and thus is not harmed in being deprived by her of a benefit to which it is not entitled. Kamm does not consider whether a fetus is harmed or made worse off when a woman delays having an abortion, relative to the prospects it had before she delayed. Kamm's arguments allow her to justify most abortions, including those in late pregnancy. Like many philosophers, she finds the viability cutoff problematic, and she suggests, like Gert, that viability may be relevant because, when a fetus is viable, there may be a way at little extra cost to the woman to discontinue support without killing the fetus.[39] But if viability is relevant in this way, then the state should only restrict the abortion method used (e.g., a feticidal vs. a nonfeticidal method), not pregnancy termination.

Jeff McMahan criticizes Kamm's defense of abortion. He argues that a person has a special obligation to aid someone if she has caused that person to require her aid in order to avoid serious injury or death.[40] McMahan's principle is a version of Regan's third exception under which a person has a duty to help those endangered by her action. McMahan then argues that because the woman and her partner's actions have caused the fetus's existence, even if unintentionally and even if she acted responsibly in doing so, she and her partner have jointly caused a person to require nine months of her bodily support in order to avoid death. Therefore, they are jointly obligated to provide the aid the fetus requires to avoid death. McMahan argues, contra Kamm, that they are responsible even if they could have avoided this situation only at considerable cost to themselves, such as abstaining from all heterosexual intercourse. McMahan acknowledges that the obligation to aid the fetus will fall on the woman, as her equally obligated partner cannot provide the bodily support the fetus requires. Yet he suggests that the partner can fulfill his obligation by giving aid to the woman while pregnant or giving comparable life-preserving care to the infant after birth. McMahan contends that the only way to avoid the conclusion that a woman has a special obligation to the fetus is to drop the assumption that the fetus is a person. For the moral principle McMahan invokes—that person A has a special obligation to aid person B when A has caused B (even unintentionally and while acting responsibly) to need A's help in order for B to avoid death—applies only to persons.

McMahan's principle purportedly undermines a major premise of Kamm's argument: that a woman has no special obligation to the fetus. Yet McMahan's principle would seem to require that parents provide whatever aid is necessary for their children to avoid serious injury or death. For example, if a child required not nine months of gestation but a new kidney or a heart at age ten to avoid death, and only the parents' kidneys or hearts were available or genetically compatible, then because the parents' actions caused the child to need their help (by bearing and raising it), the parents would be required to donate a kidney or heart. Presently U.S. laws do not require parents to give even blood or bone marrow to their children, let alone vital organs. Of course, perhaps our laws should require this, and I would gladly support legally requiring parents to provide the blood or bone marrow necessary to perform health- and life-preserving therapies on their children. But providing small amounts of blood or bone marrow is significantly less burdensome than a pregnancy, and providing a heart or even a kidney is more burdensome than a healthy pregnancy.

McMahan does not actually hold that parents owe unlimited or costly help to their biological offspring and therefore suggests that we drop the assumption that the fetus is a person in order to save Kamm's arguments. But if we drop this assumption, then McMahan has no basis for holding that a pregnant woman has any duty to help a fetus, even a minimal one, such as avoiding cocaine or heavy alcohol use or continuing a healthy pregnancy that has reached seven months. However, Kamm's notion of a "good enough parent" may help her avoid the extreme consequences that appear to follow from the fact that a woman caused the fetus to need her help, without dropping the assumption that the fetus is a person.[41] For example, a woman who smokes or drinks moderately during pregnancy may meet the "good enough parent" standard, though not the ideal parent standard. The woman who smokes crack, however, probably falls below the minimum standard for childcare. Similarly, the parent who refuses a heart or kidney donation probably meets the "good enough parent" standard, though not the ideal parent standard. The parent who refuses a donation of blood or bone marrow to his or her child, however, probably falls below the minimum obligation of a parent. Similarly, a good enough pregnant Samaritan (whose duties probably fall below that of the parent, as she may not have agreed to parent) does not have an abortion at seven months unless continuing the pregnancy would threaten her life or long-term health. She probably does not have an abortion at five months without good reason, such as a severe fetal illness, or significant personal health reasons. Even at four months she probably does not have an abortion, unless she could not arrange one earlier or she has good reasons, such as the reasons already stated, or the pregnancy places her in serious emotional or economic jeopardy. Statutes requiring the levels of help suggested by these cases would command only minimally decent Samaritan services from women and not good Samaritan service. To avoid singling out women for basic Samaritan service, the state could impose comparable aid obligations on others, for example, by passing laws that require a minimum amount of child support and/or pregnant partner support from men or that require blood and bone marrow donations from parents for their children. Similarly, the state could prohibit immoderate alcohol use by fathers and not just pregnant women. In sum, moderate abortion regulations do not violate a woman's equal right to deny help in a legal context that requires minimally decent Samaritan service from all citizens.

Equal Protection from Nonconsensual Invasion | The right-to-refuse-to-help defense is often challenged by those who view an abortion not as the omission of an act that could save a life but as the commission of an act that ends a life. The commission of a deliberate life-depriving act is harder to justify than the omission of a live-saving act. Deliberate life-depriving acts are regarded as justified only when done in self-defense, in defense of one's community or nation, or to punish someone for an especially horrible crime. By contrast, refusals to help save a life are regarded as justified so long as one does not fit one of the exceptions that Regan identifies. To respond to critics who see abortion as a deliberate life-taking act, some defenders of abortion rights represent abortion as an act of self-defense.[42] A woman who has an abortion is defending herself against the potential injuries, pain, and deprivation that the fetus's occupation of her uterus can cause.

The self-defense abortion defense has some serious weaknesses. First, some challenge the idea that a normal pregnancy threatens serious bodily harm of the sort that would justify taking a person's life.[43] Second, even if an abortion can be justified as a desperate act of self-defense against an unwanted intruder who threatens serious harm, it does not follow that the abortion provider is permitted to assist a woman in her defense by removing and killing the intruder. For the fetus is not threatening the abortion provider, it is innocent of criminal intent, and its occupation of the woman is also an act of desperation to preserve its life. Nancy Ann Davis has argued that while a woman has the right to give priority to saving her own life and health over the fetus's, the physician does not necessarily have the same right to give priority to the woman's interests.[44] Third, even if pregnancy poses a threat of serious harm, the threat is not usually an immediate one. Thus, an unwanted pregnancy does not present a typical self-defense situation in which the victim is permitted to use deadly force to protect herself.

Eileen McDonagh tries to get around some of the weaknesses of the self-defense strategy by combining it with an equal protection defense. For McDonagh, abortions are not merely women's acts of self-defense against fetal invaders, instead they are part of the state's use of force in the equal defense of its citizens against attack or invasion by other human agents.[45] McDonagh argues that a state that offered protection to its citizens from injuries caused by other agents but failed to assist women seeking abortions would thereby be treating women unequally.[46] Such a government would be, in essence, permitting fetal persons to exploit, assault, invade, rape, or enslave women's bodies. The state does not tolerate these actions when they are committed by born individuals and will assist victims in stopping such assaults. Therefore, McDonagh argues, the state must equally assist women who are the victims of a fetus's unintentional exploitation.

Unlike the woman or abortion provider, the state has the authority both to determine whose legally protected interest or right will prevail and to use deadly force to uphold the law. McDonagh contends that the state should give greater weight to a woman's rights and interests in a situation of unintended pregnancy, because the fetus's act, though desperate and unconscious, uses a woman's body without her consent. The fetus's act therefore counts as an act of invasion, assault, rape, colonization, and enslavement. The state must stop the fetus's invasion, assault, and rape by providing a woman abortion services, even if as a result the fetus will be killed. The medical professionals who provide abortions, on McDonagh's account, are simply the officials to whom the state has delegated the authority to enforce the law. Moreover, although McDonagh appears to regard the bodily changes that take place in a normal pregnancy as a form of serious bodily harm, she argues that the state should protect citizens from any unwanted use of their bodies, whether the use could result in a serious injury or not. Thus, a pregnancy need only qualify as unwanted bodily use in order to justify the state's use of force to remove the unwanted occupant.

McDonagh's arguments challenge abortion opponents who represent abortion as a deliberate life-depriving act, as the self-defense argument is designed to do. Her arguments handle the objection that most pregnancies do not involve bodily harm serious enough to justify a life-depriving act by the potential victim or a third-party assistant in that, to justify lethal self-defense, a pregnancy need only constitute a nonconsensual use of another's body. Moreover, her arguments justify third-party assistance by invoking the state's authority to adjudicate conflicts of interest and use deadly force in the defense of persons whose bodies are occupied nonconsensually. And by equating abortion with an act encompassed by the state's enforcement of the law and the government's duty to protect citizens, the fact that the threat of harm is not immediate is not an issue. This is because an abortion is not an act by an individual who takes the law into her own hands in self-defense.

Furthermore, because McDonagh represents authorizing abortions as part of the state's obligation to equally protect citizens from assault and injury, the provision of abortion services is something that any liberal government should do.[47] That is, on McDonagh's view, state funding for abortion providers would be equivalent to state spending on its domestic police force. McDonagh notes this feature of her account and writes that "the captive samaritan basis for abortion rights, in contrast to the bad samaritan one, clarifies what is at stake in the issue, thereby gaining for women the right not only to an abortion but also to abortion funding."[48] The right-not-to-be-a-captive defense does so by representing state-funded abortions not as public charity but as obligatory state protection in a liberal society.[49]

In addition, McDonagh's abortion defense gets around the usual objections to self-defense justifications without treating the fetus as a nonperson. McDonagh does not merely grant the personhood of the fetus for the sake of argument, as those who defend the right to be a bad Samaritan do; her view depends on viewing the fetus as a separate human agent (albeit an unconscious and incompetent one). McDonagh writes: "To the degree that the fetus shares the attributes of a person, its imposition of normal pregnancy against a woman's will is an invasion of her right to be let alone from other private entities."[50] If being pregnant were more like suffering from a nonhuman threat such as a flood or an animal bite and less like being the victim of another human agent's unwanted embrace, we would be less entitled to the state's police protection. As McDonagh's writes:

If the fetus is a bunch of alien, nonhuman cells, then the state must not omit funds for abortions from health-benefit policies or if, however, the fetus is state-protected human life, then the state must fund abortions as part of its police power, which provides law and order, a power that includes stopping human life from causing harm by intruding on the bodily integrity and liberty of others.[51]

In brief, McDonagh's right-to-avoid-captivity defense justifies police protection only if the kidnapper is a person, even if it is barely a kid itself. In a more recent publication, McDonagh concedes that a fetus may be analogous to state-protected nonhuman life, in which case women would have the same right to state-funded protection as they would if they were attacked by a wolf or grizzly bear.[52] Yet if the fetus is only protected nonhuman life, then her view that state sponsorship of abortions fulfills the state's obligation to equally protect women from assaults by other citizens is substantially weakened. The state seems to have a lesser obligation to protect us against wildlife or natural disasters and events, and when it does so, as McDonagh suggests, the state provides healthcare benefits or disaster relief, not police power.

Yet McDonagh does not view pregnancy as a "natural event" but as a violent and unintentionally criminal act. McDonagh configures the pregnant woman as a victim of assault, kidnapping, rape, and enslavement, and thus the fetus is rendered an assailant, kidnapper, rapist, and enslaver. Though her arguments do not dehumanize the fetus or degrade its moral standing, they demonize and criminalize the fetus. Borrowing from the language of law and criminology, she takes what some feminists have called "the two hostile persons"[53] view of pregnancy to new heights. McDonagh writes:

It is *conflict* that typifies a pregnancy relationship; this conflict includes the fetus's intimate imposition on a woman, which is to say, her virtual *enslavement* by it.

If a woman does not consent to pregnancy, the fetus has intruded on her liberty in a way similar to that of a *kidnapper* or *slave master*.

A woman's bodily integrity and liberty is just as violated by preborn life that implants itself, using and transforming her body for nine long months without consent, as she is when a born person massively imposes on her body and liberty without consent, as in *rape, kidnaping, slavery, and battery*.[54]

The primary purpose of these violent mataphors is to render abortion a legitimate, state-sponsored use of deadly force, as is evident in the following passage: "Preborn human life is a powerful *intruder* upon a woman's body and liberty which *requires the use of deadly force* to stop by removing it."[55] While rape, kidnapping, battery, and slavery are inherently violent practices, to treat the fetus's nonconsensual use of a woman's body as similar to these seems to trivialize the latter. Robin West points out, in her discussion of McDonagh's book, that:

> Even acknowledging the profound alterations of a woman's physical body occasioned by a normal pregnancy . . . pregnancy, even when nonconsensual, does not typically threaten death, lasting bodily injury, or even *an immediate* disruption of the woman's life plans and projects the way a violent assault by a born person most often does. Women who are undergoing nonconsensual pregnancies are typically *not* in fear of their lives; they don't worry that the fetus will kill them, and for a good part of their pregnancy they can go about their normal life routines.[56]

By contrast, women who are raped, kidnapped, enslaved, and battered do fear for their lives and suffer a significant loss of freedom.

McDonagh claims that judicial reasoning commonly invokes one or more of the following representations of pregnancy: (1) the incubation of new life; (2) a process of fetal growth; (3) the effect of sex; (4) a necessary burden; or (5) a woman's gift to society.[57] McDonagh argues that the first two metaphors obscure what the fetus does to a woman, as it grows and as she incubates it. The third confuses the biological cause of pregnancy—an embryo's implantation in a woman's uterus—with a social activity, sex. And the fourth and fifth serve to normalize and trivialize the physical and emotional demands of pregnancy. By contrast, McDonagh's descriptions call attention to what the fetus does to a woman when she has an unwanted pregnancy. By treating unwanted pregnancy as analogous to slavery and rape, McDonagh certainly does not trivialize what many pregnant women endure. I agree that the standard, widely circulated, metaphors for pregnancy need to be contested, but McDonagh's metaphors are equally problematic. Not only do they trivialize rape and slavery, but by misrepresenting abortion as an extreme response to extreme aggression, they trivialize the state's use of lethal force.

Even if we accept McDonagh's overblown descriptions of pregnancy, the state is not automatically entitled to use deadly force to defend us. If the fetus is a person, then it too is guaranteed equal protection under the laws and cannot have its life taken away without due process. What due process would amount to in the case of wrongful pregnancy is unclear. Since most abortions are not urgent, investing physicians with the authority to issue summary judgments and punishments seems unwarranted. If we are to take seriously McDonagh's suggestion that an unwanted pregnancy involves a criminal offense that may involve sanctions such as the death penalty, then we need to consider having a fair process for adjudicating such criminal charges. A fair process should established the amount of harm done, the degree of responsibility by different parties, and the appropriate punishment or remedy. Not all women are injured by an unwanted pregnancy in the same way, not all pregnancies are unwanted to the same degree, not all fetuses have used their victims for the same lengths of time, and not all cases justify a death sentence.

Perhaps it would be better if the state could resolve conflicts involving nonconsensual bodily use without resorting to lethal force. For example, suppose I discover that someone is using for her benefit an ovum, blood, or cells of mine that I've had removed from my body. If the ovum has been used to create someone else's child, we would probably not want the state to stop this unauthorized use of my genetic material by destroying the child. Similarly, if my blood or cells are being used to preserve someone's life, without my consent, we would probably not want the state to automatically stop the treatment. Each situation that requires state intervention needs to take into account a variety of circumstances, interests, and possible remedies and will draw on our sympathies in different ways. Although pregnancy involves the fetus's use of blood, cells, gametes, and so on, that have not been removed from a woman's body, we still may not want the state to stop the fetus's nonconsensual use upon a woman's request at all stages of pregnancy. If a woman requests an abortion at seven months, and she has not tried to pursue an abortion earlier, then we might want the state to find ways other than terminating a pregnancy to remedy the conflict created by the fetus's nonconsensual use of her body. By assimilating all unwanted pregnancies to acts of rape or enslavement, McDonagh's view does not allow the state to discriminate between a seven-week fetus and a seven-month fetus when it enforces the law and evicts the fetus. For, if a rape is occurring, it simply needs to stop.

In sum, McDonagh misrepresents unwanted pregnancy as a form of extreme violence against women in order to justify state-sponsored abortions. Though pregnancies limit women's freedom and opportunities and, for some women, compromise their health, to compare pregnancy with the wrongs of slavery and rape trivializes these acts and obscures the fact that unwanted pregnancies are not, by any sane stretch, acts of extreme aggression, domination, and subordination. Moreover, justifying state-sponsored abortions of fetal individuals, without a careful and difficult process of establishing the harm done, the interests at stake, the responsibilities of different actors, and the possibility of less extreme remedies, case by case, serves to normalize and trivialize the state's deployment of deadly force. Therefore, although McDonagh's "equal protection from nonconsensual use" argument avoids the objections that plague other self-defense approaches, and it creatively identifies a constitutional basis for the public funding of abortion, the analogies on which her conclusions are based carry too much problematic and dangerous baggage.

Given the problems involved in representing abortion as justified state protection or self-defense, we might want to question the assumptions that lead to this argument. Few people approve lethal forms of self-defense or law enforcement in order to protect someone's economic interests or mental health, yet many abortions are sought for these reasons. And, given that most pregnancies do not involve threats of serious bodily injury or death, we have to either approve the state's use of deadly force for more minor assaults or treat all cases of pregnancy as if they threaten serious bodily injury. McDonagh does both. Alternatively, we might question whether an abortion is a deliberate act of killing or whether it involves killing a full human being. These assumptions are difficult to challenge. However, a defense of a restricted right to abort does not require denying them completely but only modifying them.

First, abortions need not involve deliberate acts of killing, if reasonable steps are taken to avoid killing the fetus and to preserve its life whenever this is possible. In other words, if abortions are to be acts of refusing to help, and not deliberate acts of killing, then abortions should be limited to removing the fetus and not include extinguishing its life. Sometimes these acts are separable and, when they are, killing the fetus or letting it die requires additional justification. Second, in the early stages of pregnancy, the fetus is probably not a full human being, but neither is it a mere thing. Perhaps it's useful to compare the fetus to a nonreplaceable resource that has value to a community, much like a forest, nonhuman animals, works of art, historic districts, and so on. If abortions do not deliberately deprive full humans beings of life (because their purpose is fetal removal, and embryos and young fetuses are not full human beings) then a full self-defense abortion defense is not necessary. Nevertheless, these qualified assumptions raise the bar for justifying some abortions, and support restrictions on abortion somewhat more stringent than those under *Roe*. For example, they support regulations on abortion now in place in many states that define physician responsibilities to viable fetuses, and they support restricting nontherapeutic abortions to the early stages of pregnancy when the fetus is less fully human. Moreover, they support regulations that require nonfeticidal abortion methods be used whenever this can be done without raising the risks of the abortion procedure to the woman. When embryos or fetuses can be kept alive, then reasons other than the biological parents not wanting them would be needed to justify destroying them, such as the benefits to humanity of using them for research, the absence of any parents to care for them, an unacceptably low quality of life, and so on. Although my second assumption demotes the young fetus from a full human being to a nonreplaceable resource with considerable community value, there are many situations in which the owners of such goods are not allowed to destroy their property. A developer may not be permitted to develop land that provides a habitat for an endangered species, a homeowner may not be allowed to destroy a house that has historic interest, a lumber company may not be allowed to destroy a forest, and so on. As a pregnancy advances, the community's interest in the fetus increases, which should increasingly constrain what a woman is permitted to do with it. Yet, early abortions can be justified when there are social, economic, and ordinary health reasons for avoiding pregnancy and parenthood.

Bridging the Divide | Some philosophers would describe the position I am taking as the "moderate" position on abortion. According to Roger Wertheimer,

> for the moderate, the fetus is not a human being, but it's not a mere maternal appendage either; it's a human fetus, and it has a separate moral status just as animals do. A fetus is not an object that we can treat however we wish, neither is it a person whom we must treat as we would wish to be treated in return. Thus, *some* legal prohibitions on abortion *might* be justified in the name of the fetus *qua* human fetus, just as we accord some legal protection to animals, not for the sake of the owners, but for the benefit of the animals themselves.[58]

The moderate holds that the fetus is an object of value, though not equal in value or status to an adult woman. Like Dworkin, I hold that the fetus's value or status increases as the pregnancy advances. Yet some moderates attempt to determine when in the course of a pregnancy a fetus achieves a level of moral standing deserving of community protection.[59] This approach essentially ignores the burdens that pregnancy imposes on women and simply assumes that, once the fetus achieves a particular level of moral standing, these burdens are ones that we can expect a morally decent person to assume. Yet, as Regan notes, this approach cannot explain why the state should only protect a fetus in a limited way even when the required level of moral standing has been reached. Alternatively, if we focus on the woman's right to refuse a high-risk rescue, then there is no magic threshold or line in a pregnancy that, once reached, guarantees the fetus a right to life. At any point in a pregnancy, we need to balance the burdens a pregnancy imposes on a particular woman against the fetus's intrinsic and extrinsic value, such that the increasing value of the fetus requires that the burdens be more compelling at each successive stage. Furthermore, although the fetus has value, it does not necessarily have individual interests or rights, as Dworkin argues. Animals and forests have value, though not necessarily rights that compete with the rights of persons. Respecting a fetus's value and dignity because of its humanness serves a public interest. In general, the interests at stake in an abortion, other than a woman's, are public interests, such as the fair and efficient allocation of scarce medical resources, the protection of women's and children's health, and maintaining respect for the special value of human life. Thus unlike some moderates, I do not hold that restrictions on abortion should be based on the fetus's acquired rights.

I am not suggesting that the competing interests involved be invoked to adjudicate every case of abortion. Rather, I am suggesting that these principles be employed to support judicial guidelines and legislative statutes pertaining to abortion. If we take into account a woman's rights (1) to privacy, (2) to refuse to help, and (3) to destroy nonreplaceable property in which there is a community interest to serve important personal interests, as well as the various ways rights (1) through (3) are limited, then a scheme very similar to the ABA scheme I discussed in the previous chapter should seem sensible for regulating abortion. This scheme permits a period for abortion on request when the fetus has the fewest human traits, followed by a period permitting statutes banning abortions but containing broad exemptions, followed by a period in the latest stages of pregnancy permitting statutes banning abortions that contain narrow exemptions. This scheme captures what Annette Clark describes as the views of some people who fall in the moral middle on abortion, that is, people who

> believe that the timing of the abortion is the most important factor in determining its moral status. . . . The importance of timing follows from a balancing of the woman's always present interest in decisional autonomy with society's graduated valuation of human life in utero, a value which . . . increases as embryonic or fetal development advances.
>
> One possible result of this balancing is a belief that abortion early in pregnancy is a morally acceptable choice regardless of the woman's reason for wishing to terminate the pregnancy. . . . This would follow if the woman's moral claim to choose an abortion early in pregnancy outweighs the societal value of embryonic, as opposed to more fully developed human life. As the pregnancy progresses, the moral acceptability of abortion might wane in those circumstances where the woman could reasonably have made the decision to terminate the pregnancy earlier but did not. One could imagine a presumption against the acceptability of abortion beyond, say, the fourth month of pregnancy, but with the understanding that either later developments, such as diagnosis of a fetal defect by amniocentesis, or particularly traumatic circumstances such as pregnancy resulting from rape or incest, might prevent a woman from having had a reasonable opportunity to exercise her choice earlier in the pregnancy.[60]

I have tried to show that Blackmun's original time span for nontherapeutic abortion and the ABA scheme both reach a better moral balance between a woman's ongoing interest in decisional autonomy and society's gradually increasing interest in protecting the fetus as a pregnancy advances. I have also tried to show why "the moral acceptability of abortion might wane in those circumstances where the woman could reasonably have made the decision to terminate the pregnancy earlier but did not" by arguing that, in these cases, the entire course of a woman's conduct may make the fetus worse off than it would have been without her continued support.

Under an ABA-like scheme, women may abort fetuses diagnosed with disabling conditions and illnesses, though I am uncomfortable with justifying abortions on eugenic grounds per se.[61] A fetus's disability may inform a woman's decision to abort, and her assessment of her ability to assume additional care responsibilities should inform what the state counts as necessary to preserve a woman's mental or emotional well-being or economic security. Of course, her ability to assume additional responsibilities is somewhat contingent on the kind of public support a parent in this situation can expect, as the Spanish court ruling, discussed by Glendon, concedes. Moreover, our laws should take into account the potential suffering that birth or life might impose on the fetus. Nevertheless, decisions in pregnancies involving disabled fetuses could be held to the graduated legal guidelines I've proposed, so that aborting a disabled fetus in late pregnancy would be justified not in terms of preventing the birth of a disabled individual but in terms of the impact of the disability on the parents' emotional health or the fetus itself. Such criteria recognize the costs that some disabling conditions impose on their bearers or on others and do not give credibility to the idea that fetuses and children with disabilities are inherently less valuable or less deserving of our support. Challenging the presumed lesser value of disabled lives means that prenatal testing and selective abortion should be voluntary and not socially coerced.[62] Those who do not feel qualified to assume the extra responsibilities involved in raising children with various physical or mental disabilities might seek such testing, as well as potential parents who are carriers of genetic traits that could impose significant suffering on their offspring. But there is no reason to impose such testing on everyone or to assume that those who resist testing and selective abortion are irrational. In short, in the late stages of pregnancy, we should question "selective" abortions that contradict all reasonable interpretations of the idea that human life is inherently valuable. Abortions done at twenty-three weeks because the fetus is female or would face moderate physical or mental disabilities, reflect the belief that these lives are less valuable.[63] Such beliefs are unreasonable and should be challenged.

In analyzing the persistence of the abortion controversy, I have focused on alternative criteria and schemes for regulating abortion rather than simply on the justification for these schemes. Many articles that have been written revamping and rewriting *Roe* imply that the problems with this ruling could have been avoided if the justices had simply developed stronger constitutional justifications. In particular, some theorists conjecture that, had the Court employed equal protection reasoning, such as the equal right to noninvolvement, rather than privacy based reasoning, the scheme in *Roe* would have held up better to subsequent challenges. If my analysis is correct, then an equal protection defense, such as Sunstein's or Regan's, would not be sufficient to address the backlash and subsequent weakening of *Roe*. In chapter 1, I argued that the backlash to *Roe* was due not only to the legalization of abortion but also to the wide window for abortion on demand that *Roe* required states to leave open. In this chapter, I have argued that neither privacy nor equal protection requires that the window for unrestricted abortion be set at six months. Thus, replacing *Roe*'s privacy reasoning with equal protection reasoning will not necessarily shore up *Roe*'s results or scheme. Moreover, if abortions are ever understood by the public to involve the deliberate killing of full human beings, as some opponents allege, then neither privacy rights nor the right to noninvolvement will be adequate to defend most abortions. I have argued against understanding abortion as the deliberate killing of human beings, but my arguments depend on some changes in abortion practices. They also entail recognizing the fetus's increasing value and the variety of public interests at stake in a decision to destroy it. I conclude that the restrictions on abortion supported by both privacy and equal protection reasoning converge on a scheme somewhat different than *Roe*'s. I think my arguments acknowledge the legitimate concerns on both sides of this debate, and I offer them as a possible compromise in an effort to end the civil war on abortion that *Roe* escalated.[64]

From
Reproductive
Choice to
Reproductive
Barbie
The Politics
of Visibility

Casting Abortion as a "Choice" | Ian Shapiro writes that "the tasks of political theory are of two main kinds: describing and justifying the most appropriate political institutions for human beings and engaging in principled criticism of the everyday social practices engaged in within those institutions. . . . Both tasks . . . are best informed by a commitment to a democratic ethos."[1] As part of a commitment to democratic dialogue and change, in this chapter I explore how my political and moral arguments could be utilized in public campaigns for abortion rights.[2] In particular, I build on the work of feminist scholars who are both questioning the "choice" focus of mainstream feminist groups and attempting to frame new strategies. I explore the reasons for finding "choice" to be inadequate as a political tool in response the campaigns of "pro-life" groups. I also propose some rhetoric and symbols that might replace "choice" in feminist campaigns for abortion rights.

The "choice" rhetoric took center stage as privacy based reasoning proved to be successful for defending abortion rights in U.S. courts.[3] The privacy defense renders the abortion decision an individual "choice" that needs to be protected from societal interference. Privacy based reasoning is increasingly being questioned by feminist legal scholars and, accordingly, so is the rendering of abortion as a private choice. In chapter 2 I argued that, if access to safe abortion is necessary to decide what the place of sex is in our interpersonal relationships, whether to procreate, and with whom we want to associate, then abortion rights are legitimately part of privacy. Yet Dworkin's privacy defense, in which the right to abort is encompassed under the protection of religious freedom, and Regan's equal-right-to-deny-help defense provide more useful ways to understand how the right to abort should be limited. Both of these arguments offer ideas for refocusing public campaigns defending the right to abort.

Rickie Solinger attributes the hold of "choice" on reproductive politics to its appeal in a consumer-oriented culture. She writes:

> The determination of abortion rights advocates to develop a respectable, nonconfrontational movement after *Roe* encouraged many proponents to adopt the term "choice." In a country weary of rights claims, choice became *the* way liberal and mainstream feminists could talk about abortion without mentioning the "A-word." Many believed that "choice"—a term that evoked women shoppers selecting among options in the marketplace—would be an easier sell; it offered "rights lite," a package less threatening or disturbing than unadulterated rights.[4]

Associating choice with having more market alternatives, rather than having more civil and political freedom, certainly makes advocating choice less controversial. "Choice" not only implies having alternative market options but is itself one of the many good things we can buy. For example, companies, such as AT&T, sell us "choice" (figure 3.1). But

Figure 3.1
Advertisement, *Los Angeles Times*, July 5, 2001.

Figure 3.2
Advertisement, *New York Times*, July 6, 2001.

other companies, such as Verizon, offer us "life" as a choice (figure 3.2). "Pro-life" ads participate in the conflation market preferences and political demands but offer consumers "life" rather than "choice," as in their slogan: "Life—What a Beautiful Choice."[5] Because it is less threatening to contest consumer options rather than political freedoms, both feminists and their opponents equate reproductive rights with consumer privileges and tastes.

Multiplying consumer options is not necessarily a good thing if the choices are bad ones or merely replicate other options. Some "pro-life" ads cleverly expose the absurdity of promoting choice per se as a positive commodity, without reference to the content of newly offered choices. One bumper sticker proclaims "Some choices are wrong!" and reminds us that choices can be compared and evaluated. Another says "Without life there is no choice," implying that life is more fundamental than choice. The slogan "Choose life, your baby would" reminds women that they are choosing for others. And the declaration "It's a child not a choice"[6] (figure 3.3) recognizes that some things are not reducible to a

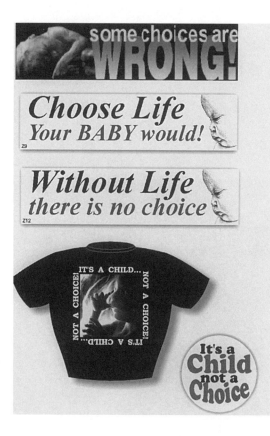

Figure 3.3
Items for sale from a "pro-life" website.

consumer choice. More graphically, posters featuring fetal corpses demonstrate that not every choice should be open to us (figures 3.4 and 3.5).[7] Given these astute observations about celebrating choice before we have defined our choices, what comeback can "pro-choice" proponents make? "Pro-life" advocates may be aware that their product is easier to market when they create slogans such as "Choose Life," which is now appearing on car license plates in many states. For what alternatives do we have—"Choose Death" or maybe "Choose Choice"?[8]

Planned Parenthood has launched a "Responsible Choices" campaign in order to promote the idea that women do make good choices when they are allowed to.[9] But surely not all women make good choices, and trusting people to make good choices does not avoid the need to make laws prohibiting some choices. The Pro-Choice Public Education Project (PCPEP) says "It's pro-choice or no choice" (figure 3.6).[10] Yet are these really our only options? Without safe abortion services women still have choices, though they may be less appealing ones. A poster from this group offers us a glimpse of what life without choice looks like. It features the image of an unattractive man (the poster is referred to as the "geek" poster) repeated many times (figure 3.7). In this

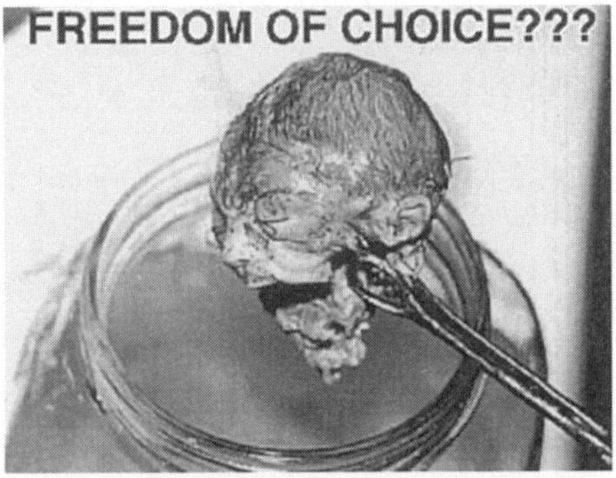

Figure 3.4
Dead aborted baby,
Lancaster Life
website.

Figure 3.5
Genocide Awareness
Project poster.

Figure 3.6
"Pro-choice" slogans.

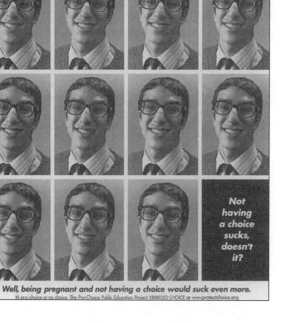

Figure 3.7
Geek Poster, DeVito/
Verdi, Pro-Choice Public
Education Project.

graphic, the absence of choice is equated with a severely depleted or regulated dating market. But is this poster about the absence of choice or simply the absence of desirable choices? If the poster featured a less geeky-looking man, say Brad Pitt, would the lack of alternatives be a problem for many young, white, heterosexual women? Kristen Luker has argued that, in order to preserve their political victories, "pro-choice" activists "must paint a vivid and frightening picture of what the future will be like if the opposition is successful." Moreover, she contends that the "pro-choice" movement must "convince its own members that the pro-life movement is a serious threat, against which all available resources must be mobilized quickly."[11] Abortion rights groups, such as the PCPEP, seem to be following Luker's advice, painting a picture that is especially frightening to the consumers they want to reach.

Discussing the visual propaganda of the abortion debate, Maud Lavin writes:

> In our highly individualistic culture, propaganda and advertising usually emphasize personal choice whether it's choice among brands of shampoo, types of cars, or the slants of political candidates. In this case, the visual repetition of portraits of fetuses and to some extent mothers has worked to pin the abortion debate's issues tightly to individual rights.[12]

The individual rights at issue are not simply consumer rights but the political and civil rights I discussed in chapter 2. Lavin notes how the imagery draws our attention to either the fetus's rights or the woman's rights and obscures the social conditions that make life and choice possible. For example, the primary visual icon of the "pro-choice" movement has been a coat hanger, an object that is supposed to remind us of what women may do when they lack rights (figures 3.8–3.11).[13] The coat hanger insists that women must have liberty or they will die. Access to safe abortion is necessary so that women are not forced to make desperate choices. By contrast, the primary visual icon of the "pro-life" movement is the fetus, an image that insists that what is destroyed in an abortion has rights. Macabre images equating intentional abortion with infanticide, bad mothering, and even ethnic cleansing and lynching (figures 3.12, 3.13)[14] make us wonder whose rights we should protect—the woman's or her fetus's. Many in the "pro-choice" camp are now questioning the coat hanger's success in promoting women's rights, compared to the success of the fetus image in promoting the rights of fetuses. A student recently told me that, until he was in col-

Figure 3.8
Artist unknown,
"Surgeon General's
Warning: Seek
Abortion Information
From Your Physician,"
silkscreen, ca. 1990,
Center for the Study of
Political Graphics.

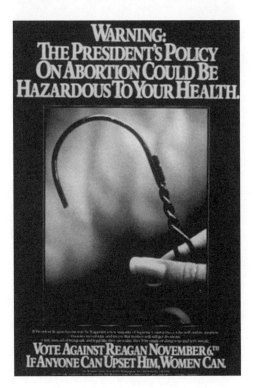

Figure 3.9
Women's Trust, offset,
1984, Center for the
Study of Political
Graphics.

Figure 3.10
Seventies poster,
DeVito/Verdi,
Pro-Choice Public
Education Project.

Figure 3.11
"Abortion Happens,"
"Pro-Choice" poster.

Figure 3.12
Protester at Denver
Planned Parenthood
Clinic, June 28, 2000.
AP photo/Ed Andrieski.

Figure 3.13
Genocide Awareness
Project poster.

lege, he was under the impression that the standard way to perform an abortion was with a coat hanger; that is, he evidently thought that, in legal abortions, the curved end of the coat hanger was used to pull the fetus out. Although this student identified himself as "pro-choice," the image of the coat hanger triggered in his mind an image of violence to fetuses, not harm to women. The meaning my student derived from the coat hanger is reflected in a "pro-life" poster that appropriates the hanger (figure 3.14).[15] In this poster, the coat hanger suggests that a back-alley abortion has two victims, and therefore that the horror, or rights violations, involved in back-alley abortions cannot be addressed simply by changing the surgical instrument.

The war over abortion has been fought not only with images but with other artistic media as well. Talented rap singers, hip-hop artists, and reggae stars have written angry, sad, and admonishing lyrics about the evils of abortion.[16] Grassroots organizations have produced dramatic and compelling films and videos depicting miniature humans at life's beginning or brand new people who are already the victims of our society's ills.[17] Political dissidents have staged emotional street protests, with babes-in-arms cast as "American holocaust survivors"

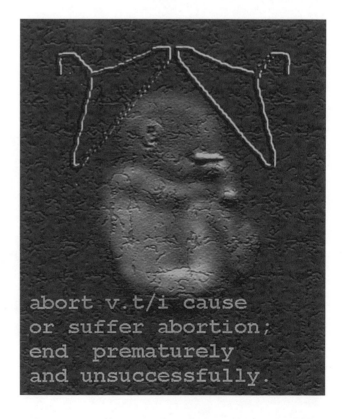

Figure 3.14
Preventing a Beethoven? "Pro-life" poster.

(allegedly children born after *Roe v. Wade*), set against poster-size photos of "American holocaust victims."[18] Painters have composed images that compare women's health centers to death camps and draw the attention of a public that is increasingly informed about genocide atrocities (figure 3.15). On the internet, voice-over baby cries haunt photo galleries featuring fetal corpses.[19] Exploiting the conventions of horror, tragedy, folk narrative, and guerilla art, antiabortion productions provide epic dramas about lives in crisis and societies on the verge of destruction. "Pro-choice" liberals and social progressives are right to question whether the coat hanger, in all its permutations, can compete with the creative efforts of political conservatives and religious traditionalists. In "The Folk Song Army," Tom Lehrer sang: "Remember the war against Franco / That's the kind where each of us belongs / Though he may have won all the battles / We had all the good songs."[20] Women's rights advocates have so far won the major legal battles on abortion, but the "fascists" opposing them appear to have the good folksongs and artwork on this issue.[21]

For more than a decade now, feminist scholars have studied the cultural weapons of the antiabortion movement in order to understand

Figure 3.15
Peter Frega, "The American Holocaust," print, 1998.

why they are effective and to mobilize appropriate responses. As far as I can tell, this scholarship has not generated substantially new rhetorical tools and uses of artistic media to defend abortion rights. In this chapter, I provide an overview of feminist scholarship on the "pro-life" movement's visual propaganda and the calls for action such studies have produced. I analyze why these calls for action have not yet been answered. I also examine artwork addressing abortion produced by feminist artists and activists. I propose ways to develop this body of feminist artwork into public campaigns that move away from "choice" and focus on the forms of help we should expect from individuals and our society. This is the issue that needs democratic debate. I agree with Lavin, who writes:

> We need to discuss and create visual propaganda about the follow-ing issues—family allowances, adoption, health care for families of all classes, caring for children with disabilities, enforcement of child-care payments, and equal pay for women. These are key reproductive-rights issues that inform the choice of whether or not to carry a pregnancy to term.[22]

Lavin's issues are about social responsibility, or the forms of social se-curity a society should put in place. These forms of social security in-form not only our personal choices but also the constraints on indi-vidual choice that citizens collectively choose to impose. In short, if the struggle for reproductive rights is not so much about removing legal barriers that make coat hangers necessary but about creating social pro-grams that offer us good, but not necessarily every, choice, then de-fenders of abortion need to jettison the coat hanger image and develop new rhetorical tools.

The Invention of Fetal Autonomy | In 1984, Rosalind Petchesky called attention to a significant shift in the justificatory language and conceptual tools of antiabortion groups in the decade following *Roe v. Wade*.[23] By the mid-1970s, the predominantly Christian "pro-life" movement began to pursue its legal and social agenda by invoking sci-entific authority to defend an essentially modern Catholic doctrine about the beginning of life. Politically savvy abortion opponents began to discuss abortion not merely as a failure to understand and obey the will of God but also as a form of ignorance about the workings of na-ture. They raised objections to abortion not in terms of the proliferation of unbaptized souls but in terms of the human qualities of society's most vulnerable members.[24] To demonstrate the human qualities of "the unborn," abortion foes began amassing and circulating pictures of fetuses caught in the gaze of the latest biological and medical science. By aggressively marketing and publicizing the fetus, as with the television broadcasting of *The Silent Scream*, "the fetus rose to instant stardom," according to Petchesky.[25] Petchesky's work showed that antiabortion groups have succeeded in changing common understandings of pregnancy and abortion, although these groups have failed in their ultimate legislative aims. Ultimately she demonstrated that the representation of abortion as a mortal struggle between a fetal individual and a woman has a relatively recent history, although a potentially dangerous future for abortion regulation in the United States.

Petchesky was one of the first feminist scholars to call attention to "the cultural guerrilla warfare against abortions" and the need to oppose it.[26] In 1987, she argued that "we have to restore women to a central place in the pregnancy scene. To do this, we must create new images that recontextualize the fetus, that place it back into the uterus, and the uterus back into the woman's body, and her body back into its social space."[27] However, feminist activists and artists have been slow to develop new reproductive images that displace the powerful fetus. In 1995, the feminist art critic Lucy Lippard observed that "no new icons have emerged. The fetus still reigns. We have to get the little bugger on our side, transform its unborn bathos into the misery of the unwanted child as well as the horrors of the exploited woman's body."[28]

Like Petchesky, Lippard noted both the relative impoverishment of "pro-choice" imagery and the need to revisualize reproduction. Yet, whereas Lippard favors images of miserable children or exploited female bodies, Petchesky proposed less negative images to represent the issues underlying abortion. Petchesky writes: "The strategy of antiabortionists to make fetal personhood a self-fulfilling prophecy by making the fetus a *public presence* addresses a visually oriented culture. Meanwhile, finding 'positive' images and symbols of abortion hard to imagine, feminists and other prochoice advocates have all too readily ceded the visual terrain."[29] Petchesky's primary suggestion is to place "the little bugger," as Lippard dubs it, inside women's bodies in order to create women-centered images of pregnancy that will challenge the fetus-centered ones wielded by "pro-life" advocates.

Following Petchesky, a working group at the Centre for Contemporary Cultural Studies in Birmingham, England, called the Science and

Technology Subgroup, documented the use of scientific fetal imagery in the propaganda of "pro-life" groups in England. In the late 1980s, there was an unsuccessful campaign to approve a bill in the British Parliament prohibiting abortions after eighteen weeks of pregnancy. In introducing their analysis of the public and legislative debate over this bill, the members of this working group comment that their project "was undertaken because of our conviction that, although feminists have won short-term gains, we fear we may be losing the larger struggle over commonsense assumptions about abortion."[30] Observing some of the ways feminist strategies have failed, the working group notes: "In pitting the right to choose against the right to life, feminists run the risk of losing public sympathies, and being constructed as self-indulgent and irresponsible."[31] The reflections of this group highlight the need to reexamine the reproductive rights movement's defense of abortion, especially late abortion, in terms of the market and political ideals of choice.

In her contribution to the working group's project, Sarah Franklin examines what she calls the "'biologization' of anti-abortion rhetoric."[32] In particular, Franklin examines how supporters of the parliamentary bill constructed "the fetus as separate, as an individual in its own right, deserving of state protection and medical attention" by appealing to the fetus's "bio-genetic uniqueness and its potential for biological growth."[33] Franklin points out that these biological criteria have come to take precedence not only over religious criteria of personhood but also over social criteria as well, such as a person's place in a kinship network or her/his potential for social growth and support. Franklin ends her essay with a call for "a new language of reproductive politics." She writes: "In order to develop terms that are woman-centred and responsive to the realities of women's lives as mothers, workers and persons in society, reproduction must be reclaimed as a social process involving social persons who are interdependent and whose right to exist is not bound up with notions of radical separateness."[34] Another contributor to the working group, Deborah Steinberg, argues that "we must challenge the construction of pregnant women as two (hostile) persons. . . . Is it not also possible to understand a pregnant woman as one person, or as Sarah Franklin has put it, 'one who becomes two,' but is still one in that becoming?"[35] Franklin's and Steinberg's comments suggest that revisualizing reproduction will involve not merely putting fetuses back inside women's bodies but representing the fetus as a part of a woman's body and not as a discrete entity existing within it. By visually incorporating the fetus into a woman's body, it can be viewed as biologically and socially dependent and incomplete, rather than as an independent person with interests and rights of its own. Yet what kinds of pictures will reintegrate the fetus with a woman's body in this way? Unfortunately, it's not evident how to picture the fetus as a subordinate part rather than an equal body joined to hers. Moreover, it's not evident how to picture coming-to-be as a social, and not merely biological, process. Visual images of pregnancy seem to focus our attention on concrete and visible bodies rather than on the relatively invisible processes of social reproduction. But simply placing the fetus "back into the uterus, and the uterus back into the woman's body," as Petchesky suggests and which is easier to manage, may not be sufficient to challenge the problematic "two hostile persons" view, as Steinberg points out. Petchesky's proposal can only challenge fetal-centered notions of pregnancy. Supposing we cannot fashion appropriate images, does the Petchesky-working-group approach suggest any catchy campaign blurbs—ones that can contest the fetal-person logic of antiabortion slogans, such as "Everyone deserves a birthday" or "Abortion stops a beating heart"? These questions are difficult to answer. Yet I am not entirely skeptical about the Petchesky-working-group proposal, for certainly abortion foes have demonstrated how images can transform public attitudes to abortion. Nevertheless abortion rights advocates need to have more concrete and practical proposals before taking action.

Whereas the Birmingham working group and other feminist scholars document the use of scientific imagery to influence cultural conceptions of pregnancy, Valerie Hartouni examines the cultural symbols available to interpret the fetus as imaged by science.[36] Hartouni recognizes that images—whether of fetuses alone or attached to women—do not necessitate particular readings, and she investigates how particular meanings become obvious. Using language to defamiliarize now familiar images and to detach their usual meanings, Hartouni describes

the appearance of strange and fantastic images of fetuses in bus terminals and public restrooms, as well as on billboards, magazine covers, and the evening news. These images present a prenatal entity with seemingly translucent skin, suspended in empty space or floating free, vulnerable, autonomous, and alone, sucking its thumb in some representations, raising its hand beseechingly in others. . . . Now, what this is supposed to be an image of seems obvious, and it does not appear particularly chimerical or implausible until one stops to consider that no fetus . . . simply floats, alone, in empty public space, unconnected, self-generating, and self-sufficient. Moreover, no fetus (or image) is self-evidently what it is, thus raising the obvious question: What or who exactly is this?[37]

Hartouni and Petchesky both argue that the mass circulation of obstetrical ultrasound images has contributed to the construction of the fetus as a tiny autonomous individual, a homunculus, or a little patient in need of medical services.[38] Moreover, both contend that, with the mass circulation of ultrasound images in "pro-life" videos, pamphlets, billboard ads, and bus terminal posters, this normally private creature has become a public figure. This miniature celebrity is a product not only of a voyeuristic medical culture and a media-savvy "pro-life" movement, according to Petchesky and Hartouni, but also of a society saturated with liberal individualist political discourses. The fetus represents "man" in his natural condition; a protocitizen trapped in a state of nature vis-à-vis a pregnant woman. The mass distribution of obstetrical images urges the public to bring this little guy out of the state of nature and into civil society where, with a full set of human rights, he can escape the savagery endemic to this natural state.

To challenge these interpretations of the scientific fetal image, Hartouni considers whether it is possible to recast the fetus "as a foreign presence that feeds on or off a woman's body" rather than "an individual potentially put at risk by that body?"[39] This proposal could convey, as Lippard suggests, "the horrors of the exploited woman's body," but it might also perpetuate the "two hostile persons" model of pregnancy, although one of the "persons" would have a degraded, and possibly dehumanized, status. That is, images of pregnancy that merely add back women's bodies and draw attention to how fetuses exploit them are likely to participate in the construction of fetuses as independent agents, albeit not very nice ones. Nevertheless, Hartouni's strategy of representing the fetus a parasitic "foreign presence"—a socially marginal creature threatening our well-being—offers feminist the opportunity to mobilize xenophobic images available in our culture in order to convey the horrors of an unwanted pregnancy. Following this strategy, we might conjure miniature illegal migrants and stereotyped foreign nationals, or prenatal blood-sucking aliens and menacing squatters who illegitimately claim the bodily territory of American women. Others have made similar proposals to demonize and "monster-ize" the fetus instead of the mother who aborts it. For example, Eileen McDonagh, as I noted in the previous chapter, compares the fetus in an unwanted pregnancy to an intruder, kidnapper, rapist, colonizer, enslaver, or cancer that invades or hijacks a woman's body.[40] Unfortunately, although the fetus qua foreigner, or qua criminal, offers a way to represent fetuses as socially subordinate to women, it does so only by recirculating noxious cultural symbols in order to rationalize the use of deadly state force against the fetus. Must we degrade and dehumanize the fetus in order to contest "pro-life" imagery that aims to upgrade and humanize it? Although the fetus is no angel, must we portray the fetus as the devil in disguise or a wolf in baby's clothes?

In another passage, Hartouni urges reproductive rights activists to interrupt "'the visual discourse of fetal autonomy'—developing a vocabulary of relationship that reembodies the disembodied fetal form or resituates the gestating fetus in a uterus, the uterus in a body, and the body in social relations, thereby re-membering what is otherwise dismembered."[41] This call for action combines Petchesky's imperative to "restore women to a central place in the pregnancy scene," and Franklin's desire for a "new language of reproductive politics" that reintegrates the fetus with the female body and emphasizes the social aspects of human reproduction. But it doesn't tell us how to translate their ideas into concrete strategies for contesting the discourses of contemporary science, medicine, politics, and journalism—discourses that erase women while transforming the contents of their wombs into prenatal patients and citizens. If visually stigmatizing the fetus is a questionable practice, as I am suggesting, then Hartouni's call to action moves us no further than the calls of Petchesky and Franklin. Nevertheless, Hartouni's suggestion that we pay attention to the socially acquired knowledge with which we read reproductive imagery is more helpful. Whatever new images we create, we need to anticipate the cultural contexts in which they will be received, and the multiple and contradictory readings they can generate.

Karen Newman similarly questions the Petchesky-Hartouni strategy of "re-membering" or adding back women's bodies to visual representations of reproduction.[42] Newman informs us that "the presentation of the fetus as autonomous has a much longer history" than many feminist theorists realize, a history that predates by many centuries the fetal ultrasound or fiber-optic imaging from which many "pro-life" groups build their stock of images. Newman analyzes illustrations from obstetrical texts written from the thirteenth century to the present. These illustrations feature childlike people floating in disconnected uterine containers. Newman writes: "These earliest visualizations of obstetrical knowledge illustrate a core schema that was reproduced well into the eighteenth century: a uterus separated from the female body and a seemingly autonomous fetal figure."[43] Because modern visualization methods that efface women's bodies do not represent a significant break from longstanding illustration conventions, Newman questions the strategy of revisualizing reproduction to address the public's increasing preoccupation and fascination with the fetus.

Barbara Duden challenges Newman's assumption that the obstetrical illustrations of previous centuries provide illustrations of free-floating "fetuses." The models and drawings from earlier centuries of uteruses and their contents feature not the now familiar fetal figure (large head, tiny body) but rather more mature-looking children.[44] Duden points out that the interpretations attached to these medical illustrations by their contemporaries may differ significantly from our own interpretations. That is, Duden defends the idea that current scientific images and their common interpretations represent a significant break from the past. Nevertheless, although Newman may fail to recognize some interpretive discontinuities in relation to obstetrical imagery, she argues that the meanings attaching to current medical depictions of reproduction are variable and unstable. Newman claims that current obstetrical images have shifting meanings, not because of variation in viewers' cultural contexts but because ultrasound technology produces fuzzy abstractions and unrealistic-looking portraits. These abstractions, according to Newman, "unhinge" their referents, thereby creating what she calls "referential panic."[45] Diffusing this panic requires that an "expert" or technician assist a layperson in deciphering and, importantly, in humanizing the image.[46]

Newman argues that, because of their lack of realism and consequent referential ambiguity, obstetrical ultrasound imagery may actually be helpful for the defense of abortion. This is because nonrealistic, fuzzy ultrasound images do not obey the classical conventions of visual representation, through which an image appears to recreate the perspective of an observing subject on an object, a human perspective that then guides the meaning of the image. Because an ultrasound image is not treated as a realistic representation of what some illustrator saw, interpreters need not access the illustrator's perspective, and a space is opened for others to interject what they see in the image. Given the interpretive openness of the image, Newman concludes that:

New forms of visualization occupy at the very least an uneasy position in the contemporary debates about reproduction. On the one hand, the New Right's deployment of these fetal images, as in *The Silent Scream*, the anti-abortion film purporting to record an abortion; the constitution of fetology and obstetrics around the fetus as an individual in need of diagnosis and treatment . . . all these factors collapse the mimetic and the simulated on behalf of a humanist hermeneutics enabling to "pro-life" rhetoric.

. . . On the other hand, the new visual apparatuses can potentially be harnessed to counter classical and Renaissance modes of representation, thus disrupting the cultural logic of individualism that relies on perspective—the rationalization of sight—and an observing subject interpellated to humanize such simulated images.

The Right's insistent inscription of fetus as "baby" and feminist demands to restore the woman's body to obstetrical representation *both* display a profound humanist nostalgia for the realist image.[47]

In short, the Petchesky-Franklin-Hartouni proposal reflects a naïve realism about images and therefore misunderstands the potential social impact of new scientific imagery.

In a realist framework, the fetal image proves the reality and value of the fetus and, likewise, images of women's bodies confer greater ontological status on women.[48] Instead of generating new imagery containing women, Newman proposes that we attempt to challenge the public's desire for realistic images, especially for scientific images that presume to give us the world as it is. Unfortunately, Newman says no more about how to challenge our "profound humanist nostalgia for the realist image" and the corresponding conviction that some images can provide us direct access to reality. Moreover, she also seems to ignore the practical challenges of empowering patients to contest the control that technical and scientific experts wield over the meaning of the ultrasound image. Furthermore, the fuzziness of the ultrasound image may just be a technological phase. There are now three-dimensional fetal ultrasound images that provide a more realistic-looking portrait (figure 3.16).[49] When these are in mass circulation, it will be more difficult to treat obstetrical ultrasounds as referentially ambiguous abstractions and to neutralize the public's desires for fetal images that expose the realities of pregnancy.

Figure 3.16
Fetal face, 3D
Ultrasound.

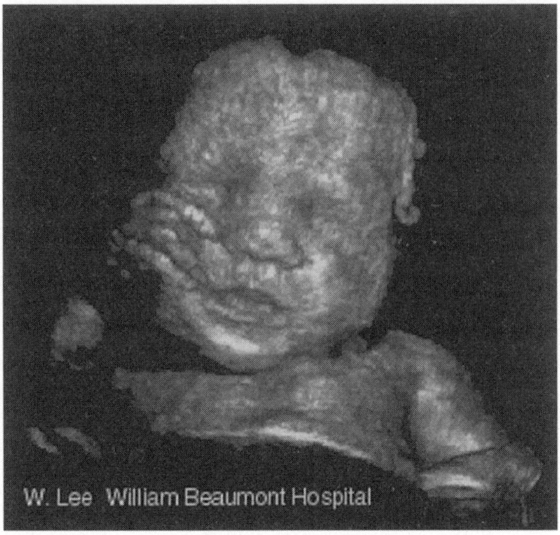

W. Lee William Beaumont Hospital

Contra Newman, then, wielding interpretive power over scientific imagery of reproduction, such as the new and improved ultrasound images, may be impractical. Yet, *contra* Petchesky and others, replacing fetal images with more "realistic" women-centered images of pregnancy reflects a simplistic realism toward images. Moreover, the pursuit of greater visual realism assumes that there is a single best way to represent pregnancy, which is absolutist and ethnocentric, as Lynn Morgan points out.[50] But can we recoup these strategies while avoiding their problems? For example, can we develop new images of reproduction, as Petchesky suggests, but create images that challenge the public's desire for scientific realism, as Newman suggests? Such images would not attempt to offer more "realistic" representations of pregnancy but would attempt to call attention to how reality, as well as the devices for representing reality, are shaped by culture. In the last section of this chapter, I offer some images that parody "pro-life" representations of pregnancy in order to contest their presumption to give us pregnancy as it really is.[51]

In developing new images, it will be necessary to reexamine how contemporary obstetrical visualization technologies have influenced the abortion debate. Lisa Mitchell and Eugenia Georges, for example, have compared common interpretations of ultrasound images in Canada and Greece and have found that "in Canada, ultrasound is about the separation and reconnection of individuals," whereas "in Greece . . . fetuses remain relational beings whose personhood is constituted primarily through social networks."[52] Importantly, in the Greek context, the prevalence of ultrasound has not given rise to public fetuses or to virulent, antiabortion rhetoric but, instead, this technology is associated with the Western modernity of the women who use it. By contrast, in Canada, like the United States, obstetrical ultrasound has contributed to the production of autonomous prenatal patients. (Not surprisingly, a recent *New York Times* headline reads: "Canada Sees Abortion War Turn Violent, Services Fall.")[53] Mitchell and Georges's ethnographic work demonstrates that the cultural context in which ultrasound is used may be more significant in shaping the public's antiabortion sentiments than the "raw" technology itself. This comparative work underscores Jana Sawicki's warning "to avoid reducing patriarchal domination to its technologies."[54]

Similarly, Janelle Taylor has found that ultrasound plays a role in constructing the fetus both as a person from the earliest developmental stages and as a product or commodity, subject to quality control and, ultimately, abortion if it is found to be defective.[55] Taylor analyzes particular justifications given for ultrasound use in U.S. medical contexts. She claims that although some practitioners appeal to the general psychological benefits of reassuring pregnant women that their fetuses do not have any health problems,

> the only medical justification for ordering the examination in any individual case is the reasonable suspicion that it *will* reveal problems, and one of the primary justifications for offering ultrasound screening to all women on a routine basis is the expectation that fetuses exhibiting anomalies will be aborted. Medical articles on ultrasound explicitly make this link between "reassurance" and selective abortion, especially in connection with cost-benefit assessments.[56]

In medical practice, ultrasound is not about proving the reality and value of the fetus but about screening the fetus for health defects and aborting it when it doesn't pass. Paradoxically, ultrasound imaging participates in constructing the fetus both as a prenatal patient deserving societal protection and as an object that must meet certain production standards and ideals before it has the right to continued support. Although the latter view of the fetus is more conducive to the goals of abortion defenders, it leads to the promotion of abortion in cases many feminists find hard to tolerate, such as sex-selection abortions and the abortion of most fetuses with disabilities.[57] In short, the fetal image, as produced by science and deployed in different contexts, has no single or inevitable impact on the abortion debate.

Visibility Politics | Consider a page from a children's fan magazine for consumers of Beanie Babies (figure 3.17). The magazine packages information for juvenile readers like an investment firm promoting stocks and mutual funds to potential buyers. Relevant quantitative data are presented by bar graphs that plot a commodity's price history and projected future value. Presumably, the child-reader of *Mary Beth's Beanie World* analyzes the financial data presented here in order to make an informed decision about what "plush toys" she or her parents should purchase. If it seems absurd to suggest that investment considerations, let alone current market price, have much influence on a child's consumption patterns, then what are these bar graphs doing here?

Bruno Latour has argued that scientific advances are made not by individuals grasping or formulating new ideas but by the practice of amassing and arraying inscriptions—that is, representations in two-dimensional and sometimes three-dimensional space of what is not present.[58] By using visual technologies, such as photographs, maps, graphs, models, and, now, hypertext documents retrievable on the internet, intellectual opponents support, defend, and argue for and against particular views and positions. Images and inscriptions, according to Latour, provide a

> unique advantage . . . in the rhetorical or polemical situation. "You doubt of what I say? I'll show you." And, without moving more than a few inches, I unfold in front of your eyes figures, diagrams, plates, texts, silhouettes, and then and there present things that are far away and with which some sort of two-way connection has now been established. I do not think the importance of this simple mechanism can be overestimated.[59]

The importance of this simple mechanism for the abortion controversy is suggested in Meredith Michaels's remark that "by the time of the *Roe v. Wade* decision, visibility had already begun to displace viability as an ontological measure."[60] Michaels's comment implies that eventually the state's interest in and protection of human life will begin the moment the fetus can be brought before our eyes (i.e., conception).

Like Latour, Barbara Duden observes that "Certain graphics convincingly create the illusion that abstract notions have a tangible

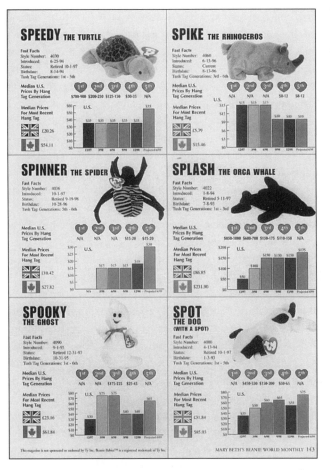

Figure 3.17
Page from *Mary Beth's Beanie World*, 1999.

reality. . . . Graphs in a newspaper advertise the rationality of an 'objective' view."[61] For instance, it may be hard for some to see the financial value of bags (admittedly cute bags) of plastic beans, but graph after graph rendering visible the absurdly high prices some customers have paid for Beanie Babies help parents, if not children, rationalize the purchase of dozens of toys. The graphs transform consuming practices into investing and saving practices. Beanie "collectors" circulate the knowledge they obtain from the graphs, which further lowers their inhibitions on spending. Duden writes: "Now, we see what we are shown. . . . This habituation to the monopoly of visualization-on-command strongly suggests that only those things that can in some way be visualized, recorded, and replayed at will are part of reality."[62] The Beanie Baby marketing phenomenon, which transformed cheap, mass-produced items into rare "collectibles" is an example of how a clever array of inscriptions can render real and rational what is very questionably real (the rarity and value of cheaply produced beanbag toys) and doubtfully rational (wealth accumulation through Beanies). Beanie consumers see, in their piles of plastic beanbags, what they have been shown.

Duden shows how the "habituation to the monopoly of visualization-on-command" currently works in favor of "pro-life" proponents. We see what we are shown and what we are shown is the fetus: a human-looking, baby-resembling, childlike fetus, or the abused and murdered fetus. The fetal image is persuasive. According to Faye Ginsburg, "the idea that . . . confrontation with the visual image of the fetus . . . will 'convert' a woman to the pro-life position has been a central theme in both local and national right-to-life activism. A popular quip summarizes this position: 'If there were a window on a pregnant woman's stomach, there would be no more abortions.' "[63] To make the public confront the visual image of the fetus, abortion foes generate what Latour refers to as "the *cascade* of ever simplified inscriptions that allow harder facts to be produced at greater cost."[64] One such "fact" is that the fetus, from the moment of conception, is biologically unique, complete, and human, and therefore a human subject with needs and claims.

The controversial website the "Nuremberg Files," which posts links to several fetus photo galleries, demonstrates the continued confidence of abortion foes in the persuasive power of the fetus image. This website offers a new, more violent, twist on the quip related by Ginsburg about how fetus exposures can convert nonbelievers. The webmasters of the "Nuremberg Files" write: "We can end the Abortion War if we ram the images of the babies being slaughtered into the minds of every citizen in this nation. Ram those images into their minds until the vast majority is ready to vomit out legalized abortion."[65] The creators of this website want to force others to ingest unpalatable images in order to chase out old opinions. Latour claims that "he who visualizes badly loses the encounter; his fact does not hold."[66] Apparently, the authors of the the "Nuremberg Files" aim to visualize well. The site opens with the words "VISUALIZE Abortionists on Trial" (figure 3.18). By depicting doctors as criminals (using clip art software) and fetuses as victims, these "pro-life" activists command us to see the criminal nature of abortion.

Can we find an image for the reproductive rights arsenal that would have persuasive power equal to the fetus? In the film *Leona's Sister Gerri*, a journalist proclaims, "What is, has always been, the answer to aborted fetuses is dead women."[67] This remark is offered to explain, in part, how a photograph taken of a particular woman, a few hours after she died from an illegal abortion, ended up in *Ms*. magazine. Evidently, the photo was used without the family's knowledge. The film explores the reactions of immediate family members to their discovery of the published photo. In the documentary, the dead woman's sister eventually reconciles herself to the political importance of its use; the woman's daughters feel its publication exploits their already violated mother. Watching the film, I find myself sympathetic to the daughters; the use of the photo by *Ms*. and other abortion rights activists exploits another woman's suffering and reduces her to a political symbol. Images of women who have died from unsafe abortions can be persuasive, but we need to be respectful toward the dead and their loved ones. Unfortunately, respectful treatment of these images means that they should not be deployed sensationally or anonymously in signs and placards, for such locations leave no room for the narrative ensuring that a woman's life is not reduced to her abortion. Yet, with an accompanying narrative, the images become more complicated, and the political message may be lost or ignored.[68] *Leona's Sister Gerri*, which

Figure 3.18
Clip art from The Nuremberg Files website.

provides many other images and details of this woman's life, partly atones for her earlier exploitation by abortion rights activists. The film itself is a useful educational and political tool, but it is unlikely to get the exposure of a photo in *Ms.* or a typical "pro-life" bumper sticker.

A poster deploying a less exploitative, although equally emotional, dead woman image features a child's drawing of a woman who died from an illegal abortion—the child's mother (figure 3.19).[69] Dead women, however, are not the only answer to aborted fetuses. As a stand-in for the dead woman, abortion rights proponents have used the simpler and possibly less manipulative coat hanger image. The coat hanger rhetorically asks: Which is the lesser evil, legal abortions or illegal abortions? This question, though, concedes that abortion is an evil, only a lesser one than the evil of giving women "no choice." Imagine a similar argument for legalizing drugs: if we don't make addictive drugs

Figure 3.19
Artist unknown,
photocopy, ca. 1986,
Center for the Study of
Political Graphics.

My mom had an Illegal abortion. I don't miss the baby I miss my mom.

Abortion must remain legal.

legal, then desperate people (addicts) will resort to more dangerous ones, or to dangerous means to get them. A "legalize drugs" campaign might deploy an image of an instrument associated with illegal drug use (for example, a dirty needle) to remind us that if we don't allow legal access to drugs, drug users will resort to back-alley drugs and dealers. This isn't a bad argument, and those who take a "harm reduction" approach defend the legalization of drugs in this way. Yet I doubt that my imagined campaign would be rhetorically effective. For if recreational drug use is assumed to be harmful or evil, in all cases, then arguing that people will use drugs recreationally no matter what society does to deter their use is not persuasive. Surely fewer people will use drugs recreationally if they are illegal, and severe measures can be taken to further discourage people from breaking drug laws, such as stiff or mandatory sentences for law-breakers. To campaign for the legalization of recreational drugs, supporters need to tackle the assumption that all recreational drug use is evil. We need not go to the other extreme and glamorize recreational drug use—surely in many cases nonmedical drug use wastes talent and health and leads to unproductive and even tragic lives. Yet using drugs, even addictive drugs such as nicotine and alcohol, is not always evil. Similarly, to campaign for abortion rights, supporters need to tackle the assumption that all abortions are evil. This is not to say that abortions are good thing, for abortions waste emerging human life, drain medical resources, and carry some, if only small, health risks to a woman. But most abortions that are performed are not evil. They represent accidents or opportunities wasted, not heinous acts.

Is it possible to change the social meaning of abortion so that it becomes associated with acts that, on balance, seem reasonable? For example, is it possible to visually and rhetorically associate abortion with responsible reproduction or the justified sacrifice of a precious resource, rather than the wrongful destruction of human life? Can we represent the evils of involuntary pregnancy, without representing the fetus as an evildoer or the pregnant woman as desperate enough to use a coat hanger? For, even if women do not resort to bad abortions, policies that impose compulsory pregnancy service on women, without giving them the means to avoid such service, are bad, and we need to have some way to show this. Carole Stabile suggests that we represent pregnancy "as work that women may, or may not, choose to undertake."[70] This seems more accurate than evoking images of slavery to characterize compulsory pregnancy, for not all involuntary work is equivalent to slavery and the fetus is certainly no slave driver. Another alternative to negative depictions of fetuses or pregnancy is to use negative depictions of violent abortion opponents. Such images could call attention to the evils of drastic infringements of privacy, rather than mischaracterize fetuses or pregnancy as inherently violent. Previous calls for imagery to diffuse the rhetorical power of the fetus image have focused almost exclusively on developing new images of pregnancy. The Petchesky-Franklin-Hartouni proposal, which I have discussed, assumes that we need to supplant the wrong view of pregnancy, reflected in the fetus image, with a better or more experientially accurate view. Yet, as Lynn Morgan argues, there is no single best view of pregnancy and thus no single best way to represent pregnancy. The negative depictions of pregnancy favored by some abortion defenders eclipse other meanings, such as the hope and joy pregnancy can signify. Moreover, as Linda Layne movingly points out, negative depictions make it hard to acknowledge or understand the pain many women experience with miscarriages.[71] Representations of pregnancy serve different ends and, whatever images we fashion, we should acknowledge their partiality and incompleteness. In short, there are other ways to visually represent the meaning of abortion than by using images that reduce compulsory pregnancy to bodily colonization, the fetus to a colonizer, and the pregnant woman to a desperate victim who will inflict self-harm if she is not allowed to kill the foreign agent who oppresses her.

Furthermore, just as abortion rights advocates should not rely on depictions of victimized pregnant bodies and women to get at the meaning of abortion, they should not rely on images that focus exclusively on the metaphysical or ontological aspects of pregnancy or fetal humans. To focus visually on the relative biological, social, or moral status of the fetus and the woman is to concede that the abortion debate rests on resolving this issue. But the moral issues raised by abortion are not entirely contingent on what kind of entity the fetus is, because there are limits to the help we are required to give others, regardless of their biological, social, or moral standing. Moreover, the fetus's status need not be static but may evolve gradually as a pregnancy develops, and the obligations a woman incurs to sustain a fetus can be calibrated to its evolving status, as well as other factors, such as the opportunities a woman has had to avoid entering a relationship with the fetus, the level of social support she can expect to receive, and so on.

In the previous chapter, I acknowledged the need for minimally decent Samaritan laws and then attempted to define the levels of help that fall below the minimally decent standard. I argued that delaying a nontherapeutic abortion for weeks and months may fall below the minimally decent standard, but that having early abortions for any reason and late abortions for reasons appropriately serious to the stage of pregnancy does not fall below the minimally decent standard. Because pregnancy and childbirth, and not only bad abortions, impose medical risks and other burdens on women, our laws need to take into account the kinds of service we can reasonably demand from potential Samaritans. In the early stages of pregnancy, when the fetus has few human traits and a woman has not had an adequate opportunity to arrange an abortion, expecting women to sacrifice their economic security, mental health or emotional well-being, and physical comfort seems unreasonable. In the late stages of pregnancy, we may expect women to endure more of these burdens (especially if they passed up opportunities to abort) but not to sacrifice their lives or physical health. The right to be no more than a minimally decent Samaritan suggests images that focus on the right to refuse to help another if the level of help required is too high.

In concrete terms, abortion rights posters might contain information calling attention to the sacrifices that some women must make to continue a pregnancy. Borrowing a model developed by the Guerrilla Girls, whose posters often educate viewers with a bold display of a few statistics, a poster might compare the chances of death from an early (medically competent) abortion with the risk of death from childbirth. Such a graphic could help get across the idea that pregnancy can impose on some women enormous sacrifices.[72] Additionally, a poster simply listing the reasons women need abortions (birth control failure; inadequate information about or access to birth control; rape; the need to delay childbearing due to age or economic situation; existing health problems, such as, cancer, diabetes, etc.; and existing family or job responsibilities) may expose the burdens pregnancy imposes on already burdened lives. These posters would not represent all pregnancies negatively, but could focus the issues surrounding abortion on how we establish limits on our obligations to help others, including fetuses. In 1991, the artist Barbara Kruger, developed a series of posters that focused the abortion debate in this way. In bus shelters in New York city, she installed a number posters, each featuring a pregnant man behind a "help" banner. Below the banner, she included text describing the opportunities or living standard the man and his family would have to sacrifice were he to continue his pregnancy (figures 3.20–3.23).[73] These posters challenge viewers to consider both the kind and amount of help

Figure 3.20
Barbara Kruger, poster,
1991.

Figure 3.21
Barbara Kruger, poster,
1991.

Figure 3.22
Barbara Kruger, poster,
1991.

Figure 3.23
Barbara Kruger, op-ed
cartoon, *New York
Times*, June 4, 1991.

we can demand of others and whether we have the same moral expectations of men as we do of women. Each man's cry for help not only provokes questions about the level of sacrifice someone in his situation should be required to make to continue a pregnancy but the sorts of help to which he is entitled from others and which might help to resolve his crisis in the right sort of way.

Earlier I suggested that negative images of violent abortion opponents, such as clinic bombers and physician assassins, could be useful for addressing issues about appropriate and inappropriate societal interference. Another tactic is to call attention to the moral hypocrisy of antiabortion groups by broadcasting their lack of political support for healthcare or social services for children. Proclaiming themselves the protectors of the weak, many abortion opponents, with their ethic of individual responsibility, oppose state-funded healthcare or outreach programs to vulnerable children. The Guerrilla Girls have a poster that addresses the hypocrisy of Republicans who want to deny women the choice to abort but who also want to deny women programs that would give them alternative choices. This poster ridicules the medical and personal choices available to women that many political conservatives are willing to tolerate (figure 3.24).[74] Another poster that attacks the hypocrisy of "pro-life" activists who claim to protect vulnerable "children" but do little to help existing children is one by the Chicago based Sister Serpents, a group I discuss in the next section (figure 3.35). Jean Schroedel has recently demonstrated that states with the most restrictive abortion laws generally have the least adequate services for children at risk.[75]

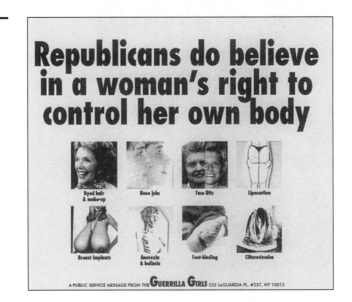

Figure 3.24
Guerrilla Girls poster, 1992.

From her research, one could compose a graphic featuring a map of the United States, that visually highlights the correlation between states that aggressively restrict access to abortion (especially for poor and young women) and states that fail to have laws protecting fetuses from third-party inflicted injuries or that fail to offer programs reaching out to abused or disabled children.

In addition, abortion rights posters could expose the hypocrisy of "pro-life" extremists who applaud the deaths of abortion providers by juxtaposing images of clinic bombings with various "pro-life" slogans (e.g., "choose life"). Lisa Link's exhibit "Warnings" includes an image that employs this tactic.[76] Her image places various "pro-life" slogans in an envelope that contains a piece of anti-Semitic hate mail typical of the threats that some clinics have received (figure 3.25). The Anti-Defamation League reports that four of the five abortion providers who have been shot by antiabortion extremists in the United States and Canada were Jewish.[77] Similarly, a poster could be created featuring an envelope containing "pro-life" buttons and anthrax, with information about the number of clinics that received letters, in the months following the World Trade Center attack, purporting to contain anthrax. Posters such as this would highlight the similarities between antiabortion extremists and other hatemongering and violent groups. In this vein, Link's "Warnings" contains images that compare the ideologies of antiabortion politicians in the contemporary United States with those of Nazi leaders. Her images juxtapose material featuring the comments of American antiabortion political leaders with artifacts documenting the persecution

Figure 3.25
Lisa Link, "Hate Mail,"
digital photomontage,
1995.

Figure 3.26
Lisa Link, "Living History," photo/ digital photo/color xerox, 1992.

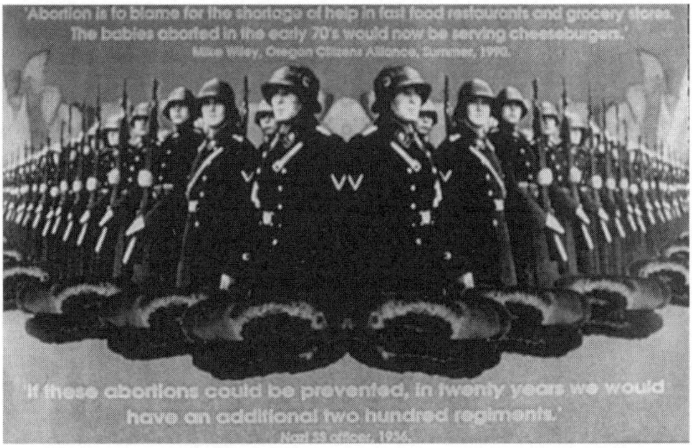

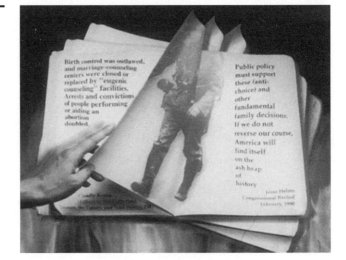

Figure 3.27
Lisa Link, "Fast Food Fodder," digital photomontage, 1993.

Figure 3.28
Lisa Link, "The Ash Heap of History," digital photomontage, 1996.

of abortion providers in Nazi Germany (figures 3.26–3.28). Lucy Lippard describes an art installation called "Heretical Bodies" (1989), by Suzi Kerr and Dianne Malley, that uses a similar tactic. According to Lippard, this installation "juxtaposed Operation Rescue leader Randall Terry's writings with the fifteenth-century witch hunter's bible, the *Malleus Maleficarum*."[78] Installations such as Link's and Kerr and Malley's implicitly question whether intolerance of abortion stems from religious and racial intolerance, and anxieties about the abortion of white, Christian "babies."

Barbara Kruger's famous "Your body is a battleground" series (figure 3.29) warns women that our bodies are contested territory and that

Figure 3.29
Barbara Kruger, billboard, 1990, and poster, 1989.

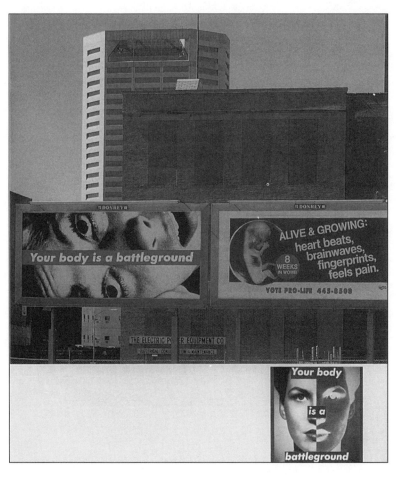

we should not take for granted the freedoms we currently have.[79] In her images, a woman's face becomes a visual field manipulated by others. The PCPEP, the umbrella organization of pro-choice groups that I mentioned at the beginning of this chapter, hired a Madison Avenue firm to create more images like these. The firm designed a series of Kruger parodies, some of which have appeared in *Ms.* magazine.[80] The PCPEP is particularly interested in reaching young women, who, according to their own research, are majority "pro-choice" but do not see abortion rights as threatened. One poster features a young woman with a pierced face, looking into the camera, and the caption says: "Think you can do whatever you want with your body? Think again." Another poster uses the curved top of a wire coat hanger to form a question mark and asks: "When your right to a safe and legal abortion is finally taken away, What are you going to do?" The "geek" poster I discussed earlier (figure 3.7) uses a large-nosed, nerdy-looking guy to horrify young, heterosexual female viewers about the realities of life without "choice." Unfortunately it also contributes to mocking men who do not conform to our society's gendered and racialized standards of attractiveness.

A more powerful, but complex, image that highlights the forces contending for control over women's bodies can be found in a street sign by the artist Ilona Granet, "A Womb of My Own," later renamed "State Womb" (figure 3.30). In this image, women's wombs are treated as government or public property, which calls attention to the totalitar-

Figure 3.30
Ilona Granet, "State Womb," 1989.

ian possibilities of "pro-life" objectives. One womb contains an image of the White House and the other contains the universal hotel symbol. Women's reproductive capacities are represented as public property and fertile grounds for various political and economic projects. To contest the illegitimate invasions of our privacy that outlawing most abortions would involve, reproductive rights posters could be developed that parody Granet's sign. These posters might feature prostrate women's bodies impregnated with other symbols of state power: flags, armies, territories, and so on. One of the images in Link's "Warnings" exhibit depicts abortion regulations that restrict the speech of healthcare providers as a form of illegitimate control over women's bodies and sexual lives. The image, "Self-Portrait with Supreme Court" (1992), features the justices and the artist snuggly under the covers of her bed, while she holds a book entitled "Gag Rule."[81] The image tells us that without information about existing reproductive healthcare services, a woman loses control over her bed, her body, and her choice of social intimates. To highlight compulsory pregnancy as a form of mandatory but objectionable patriotic service, a poster might parody a military recruitment poster, with the slogan: "Uncle Sam *wants you* to lend this embryo your uterus, heart, lungs, kidneys, and so on." Such images, like Granet's pregnant bodies or Link's invaded bed, call attention to abuses of state power rather than abuses committed by fetuses.

The Social Construction of Abortion | I argued earlier that reproductive rights proponents should avoid images of pregnancy that purport to "get at the truth" of it, as if there were a single, universal truth. Nevertheless, I think defenders of abortion should develop tools for undercutting the pretense of "pro-life" groups to possess the truth about pregnancy and abortion. For instance, in response to the common "pro-life" bumper sticker "It's a child, not a choice," abortion defenders might issue a bumper sticker that simply says, "It's not a child, it's a pregnant woman." We should create slogans that have the ring of obviousness or truth so that "our truths" will sit somewhat uncomfortably with "their truths." For example, to contest the wisdom of the advice given in figure 3.31, another sign down the freeway might read: "WARNING: Pregnancy can be hazardous to your health." In addition, images are needed that challenge the "pro-life" movement's equation of a person with a complete genetic recipe for a human body. An image by the artist Kathy High, "Follow the Chromosomes to Find Waldo," challenges the idea that having a complete set of chromosomes, or that genetic uniqueness, makes one a full human being (figure 3.32).[82] In another image, "Trangenic Fantascope," High calls attention to resemblances between fetal human bodies and fetal animal bodies. Given the resemblances between different embryonic life forms, if fetal humans are special, then it must be due to something other than their human form. Sarah Franklin describes an installation planned by the artist Helen Chadwick that was to include photographs of fetal specimens of "a horse, a hedgehog, a chimpanzee, a sloth, a pigmy, and a one-eyed boy . . . to be used as statuary emblems exploring human-animal

Figure 3.31
Billboard next to freeway in California, photo W. Furth, 2000.

Figure 3.32
Kathy High, "Follow the Chromosomes to Find Waldo," computer-generated image, 1997.

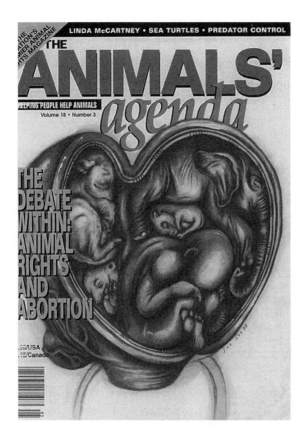

Figure 3.33
Animals' Agenda,
magazine cover,
May/June 1998.

boundaries."[83] These projects force viewers to question the fuss we make over some fetal life forms but not others.

Some viewers, of course, may conclude that animals deserve more respect and not that fetal humans deserve less. Indeed, a painting by the feminist artist Sue Coe, which compares fetal life forms, appeared on the cover of the animal rights magazine *Animals' Agenda* (figure 3.33). Inside this issue, animal rights activists explore the tensions existing between their advocacy for the humane treatment of animals and their acceptance of the seemingly inhumane treatment of fetuses.[84] Sue Coe is known for her powerful graphics depicting violence against both women and animals. One of her images depicts a gruesome gang rape that took place in a bar in Massachusetts. Another on abortion depicts the horrors of back-alley abortions.[85] Her "Dead Meat" series contains numerous images exposing the cruelties that take place daily in slaughterhouses and meat-packing plants.[86] Yet Coe's animal rights images resemble those of abortion opponents who represent clinics as death camps. Some images contain baby animals, pre- and postslaughter, such as baby chicks, piglets, lambs, and calves, and their transformation into carcasses and meat products. The familiar visual tropes are present in both Coe's images and those of "pro-life" artists: victims with numbers attached to their bodies, heaps of corpses, rivers of blood, prisonlike buildings, instruments of torture, men in lab coats, symbols of the perpetrators (the McDonald's "M" appears in *Dead Meat* in the place of the more typical swastika), and faces of especially young victims in all their innocence. In one image, ghostly cows flow in smoke away from the stacks of a Hormel plant, much like the soon-to-be-gassed fetuses that flow in bubbles toward the clinic "death camp" in Peter Frega's image (figure 3.15).[87]

Like Coe's work exposing our miserable treatment of animals, much "pro-life" art uses tools other than scientific imagery to convince us that fetuses are a misunderstood and oppressed social group. "Pro-life" artists have created visual analogies to associate abortion with known cases of human genocide and, presumably, to establish guilt by association.[88] For example, websites, such as the "American-Nazi War Memorial" or an "American Holocaust Memorial," feature images of "intolerance": the mangled bodies of victims of irrational hatreds.[89] By comparing victims, these photo compositions implicitly equate the perpetrators of these killings. Gynecologists who offer women abortion services are rendered similar to Nazi doctors and executioners. The "Genocide Awareness Project" (see figure 3.5) features tripartite posters with captions such as "Can You Connect the Dots: Extermination, Lynching, Abortion"; "Ungentile, Unwhite, Unborn"; "The Final Solution, Separate But Equal, Pro-Choice"; and "S.S., K.K.K., Planned Parenthood."[90] Each poster contains three photos: a victim of the Nazi holocaust, a victim of a racist lynching in the United States, and an aborted fetus. Abortion rights supporters could respond in kind, as I suggested earlier, with their own tripartite posters, juxtaposing images of the World Trade Center attack, the bombing of the federal building in Oklahoma, and a clinic bombing. Such visual compositions would implicitly compare extreme antiabortion activism with international and domestic terrorism.

It's hard to fault the "pro-life" movement for its horrific and manipulative images when all they seem to be doing is appropriating the techniques of good political artists. Producing images that shock, that document human suffering or expose corruption, can serve as a "wake-up" call for systemic change. Yet abortion defenders may not see the need to promote desires for fundamental change, so long as abortion is legal, and thus we may feel inclined to condemn the "pro-life" movement's shock art on abortion. There are feminists, though, who feel that a wholesale change of attitude on abortion is needed and who work in this genre. In the late 1980s, for example, a "pro-choice" poster in the shock-art mode was circulated around Chicago. A group of street artists called Sister Serpents produced a "fuck the fetus" poster (as it came to be known) and wheat-pasted it around the city. This poster displays a fetus hanging in a batlike pose with the accompanying text: "For all you folks who consider a fetus more valuable than a woman: have a fetus cook for you, have a fetus clean your house, jerk off to photos of naked fetuses, cry on a fetal shoulder, try to get a fetus to work for minimum wage, fuck a fetus," and so on.[91] Other images produced by this group express anger and frustration at the precarious nature of abortion rights, such as the image in figure 3.34, published in Sister Serpents' zine *Madwoman* from the early 1990s. A less shocking or menacing image points out the hypocrisy of antiabortion radicals who claim to be helping children (figure 3.35). A more humorous image ex-

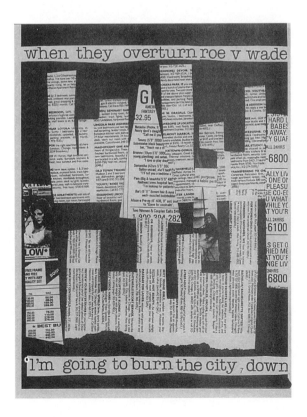

Figure 3.34
Helena Perkins, zine page, *Madwoman*, 1992.

ploits the conventions of tabloid journalism to mock the obsession of abortion opponents with fetuses (figure 3.36). Representing the intense interest that abortion foes take in women's fetuses as a form of hysteria raises questions about the sanity of these folks. In a banner that orders readers to "impregnate the fetus fanatics," the members of Sister Serpents raise questions about both the proper degree of concern for fetuses and the appropriate response to those whose concern exceeds a level that is rational.[92]

Much feminist art on abortion uses horror rather than humor or sarcasm. Kruger's "Your body is a battleground" poster, while not gruesome, invokes metaphors of war and violence. Of course, the coat hanger in all its various permutations invokes the horrors of back-alley abortions. Even an artist who appears to want to jettison the coat hanger uses macabre imagery to send it to its grave: in a recent installa-

Figure 3.35
Helena Perkins, zine
page, *Madwoman*,
1992.

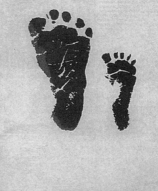

which baby benefited from operation rescue's post-natal health program ?

neither.

Figure 3.36
Artist unknown, zine
page, *Madwoman*,
1992.

tion, the "pro-choice" artist Dorothy Jiji performs a burial by placing a coat hanger in a casket on top of a grave. The tombstone inscription reads: "Hanger Died June 2 1999." Jiji's installation offers an alternative to the coat hanger symbol: a capital *C* (for choice) in the middle of a bright, blood-red circle (figure 3.37).[93] Although I am quite sympathetic to the need to bury the coat hanger and find alternative visual symbols, Jiji's proposed symbol seems to associate "choice," rather than the lack of it, with blood and death. A genuine alternative to horror tactics is to offer peaceful, nonviolent images in response to violent ones. For example, imagine cheerful images of women surrounded by their families, containing captions such as "by having an abortion at age twenty, I was able to postpone creating my family until I was ready and prepared."[94] These images would attempt to equate abortion with the exercise of women's positive agency—agency that leads to happy and productive women and well-cared-for children. In other words, rather than respond to the visual misery of abortion foes with a different kind of misery—the misery of neglected children, exploited women, or the victims of extremist violence—abortion rights proponents might respond with positive pictures of happy and productive lives enabled by the availability of birth controls that include early abortion.

The work of feminist sex workers, who advocate the right of women to control and market their bodies, may prove helpful for developing tactics that deploy both humor and shock art. For example, Carol Leigh (a.k.a. Scarlot Harlot), a sex worker and filmmaker, conducts "guerrilla street perform-ins" in which she challenges public perceptions of prostitutes as "bad women" or as criminals. Shannon Bell recounts that

> Scarlot has held public solicitations in busy downtown areas at peak pedestrian hours, most famously her 1990 public solicitation on Wall Street at lunch time. Leigh uses this tactic of guerrilla street theater to protest the soliciting laws and call for the decriminalization of prostitution. Dressed in her American flag gown, Scarlot informs the crowd: "I provide safe sex for sale and I am offering intercourse with a condom for $200. . . . I have ultimate jurisdiction over my body."[95]

Figure 3.37
Dorothy Jiji, "The Story of the Hanger," photo/A. Shrage, 1999.

In this performance, Leigh implicitly links decriminalizing prostitution with decriminalizing abortion, as she does in her Madonna parody "Pope Don't Preach, I'm Terminating My Pregnancy."[96] Many sex worker rights activists connect legal abortion and legal sex work, for both concern the right of women to use their sexual capacities for non-reproductive purposes. Typically, Leigh will stage a demonstration or "perform-in," film it to produce a "guerrilla documentary film," and then use the film as part of another performance piece.[97] By documenting the real via its performance, Leigh exposes the socially constructed nature of the real.

With the cooperation of the mass media, the "pro-life" movement does something similar. Activists create dramatic images of life and death before birth, which they display in acts of protest or civil disobedience at the entrances to abortion clinics—images that then recirculate in newspaper stories about failed "rescue missions" when the protesters are arrested. Readers of the stories might wonder why these people were arrested for trying to rescue babies like the ones in their posters. Peggy Phelan compares clinic protests to performance art and writes: "The members of Operation Rescue shrewdly understand the necessary requirements of making a spectacle and acting out for the sake of publicity. . . . These rescues tend to be emotionally and often physically violent. Like most staged rescues, Operation Rescue's demonstrations generate a feeling of terror and thereby produce the feeling that one needs to be saved."[98] In a recent interview, a clinic director speculates that her clinic "was not invaded, because it's in Queens which, from the point of view of media coverage, is geographically undesirable. They picked places in Manhattan where the media would be more likely to show up."[99] Her comment suggests that a primary purpose of clinic protests is to get the media's attention for the "pro-life" cause rather than to deter women from entering clinics. By choosing the right clinics, the theatrics of abortion opponents gain them access to the news media for the free and broad distribution of their political messages. By continually gaining the attention of the press, antiabortion performances capture the public's imagination. For a brief moment, a group of abortion rights activists took up this strategy. Brett Harvey describes an action by a group called "No More Nice Girls" that aimed to "create a vivid, outrageous and highly visible presence." The group would show up at abortion rights rallies "barefoot, chained together, and wearing voluminous black maternity garments . . . accompanied by other members of the group wearing black jumpsuits and shocking pink headbands ("commandettes"), carrying a huge pink banner which read, 'Forced childbearing is a form of slavery.'"[100] On one occasion, their performance was caught and projected by the cameras of *Life* magazine (figure 3.38).[101]

A sex worker artist and activist who uses performance art and public theatrics to defend legal pornography is the "post-*porn* modernist" Annie Sprinkle. In a piece exploring general fears about pornography, Sprinkle performs "A Public Cervix," in which, "with the aid of a speculum and flashlight [she] invites spectators to view her cervix," according to Shannon Bell.[102] Her audience members take turns holding a flashlight and gazing at her private parts. While Sprinkle wields the speculum, she converses with each spectator about "the beauty of the cervix [and] intermittently she encourages the voyeur to describe what she or he sees."[103] By exposing herself in this way, Sprinkle offers an interesting defense of pornography. Her performance shows that making visible what is normally concealed in a woman's body can both deepen our appreciation for the thing exposed and generate disgust. In this way, Sprinkle's public cervix interrogates viewers' attitudes toward

Figure 3.38
Life magazine, 1981.

both the pleasures of exposing the normally unseen and the graphic representational practices (i.e., pornography) that make such viewing possible. I find it interesting that, in her performance, Sprinkle facilitates the public viewing of the cervix not by showing ultrasound photos or medical illustrations but by providing "a bird's-eye view" of the real thing. This is what pornography purports to do with respect both to sex and to women's sexual anatomy. Sprinkle's performance challenges pornography opponents who allege that pornography makes perverse and ugly what, in its proper secrecy, is natural and beautiful. By exposing her cervix and then demonstrating that such exposures offer pleasurable forms of spectatorship without degrading the thing exposed, Sprinkle offers a counterexample to a common criticism of sexually explicit materials.

In offering her cervix for public viewing, Sprinkle facilitates the public's grasp of her cervix without visually separating or disconnecting it from her body. That is, her performance does not provide the viewer with free-floating cervix images; instead, her viewer must interact with her and her body to see a cervix.[104] Her performance helps the viewer experience the cervix as beautiful and enjoyable, while she guides and controls the viewing apparatus—the speculum. Her performance piece recalls feminist health training sessions in which a woman is offered a speculum to look at her cervix, thus usurping the authority of male doctors who enjoy privileged access to gynecological technology. Sprinkle takes this exercise a step further by actively inviting others to join her in viewing her cervix and, in doing so, takes charge of how and by whom her body is to be viewed, enjoyed, and understood.

Sprinkle's performance may give us a way to reattach the fetus to a woman's body and thereby interrogate the fetal voyeurism of the "pro-life" movement. Her work is helpful because, in producing her "post-pornography," Sprinkle does not allow herself to be objectified or eclipsed by her cervix. The viewer who wants to enjoy her cervix will find it difficult to degrade the woman to whom it belongs while viewing it, unlike the viewers who enjoy conventional pornographic images or even decontextualized fetal shots. Indeed, the latter images, mass-produced by conservative Christian "pro-life" groups, follow closely the conventions of traditional pornography, which Sprinkle is also challenging as she defends the use of porn. Feminist critics of pornography have pointed out that porn tends to reduce sex to penetration and male orgasm and to reduce sexual women to their sexed body parts. In a similar way, the free-floating fetus motif conflates reproduction with the fetal body and its transformations, implicitly treating women's bodies as insignificant and replaceable containers. Annie Sprinkle's postpornography defends porn, but it mocks the pornographer's fascination with women's sexual parts and his desire for more intimate exposures. Somewhat humorously, she provides her audience a closer close-up than traditional porn has managed. Although Sprinkle is sympathetic to the viewer's desire to see the yet unseen, she does not let this desire trivialize the woman or the body to which the hidden object is attached.

My analysis of Sprinkle's public cervix suggests challenging "pro-life" pornography by developing postpornographic representations of reproduction. These representations could expose the truly perverse aspects of free-floating fetuses and offer less degrading representations of reproduction in their place. Abortion rights artists might develop parodic reproductive imagery that could draw critical attention to what the "pro-life" movement is trying to achieve with its voyeuristic images, much the way Sprinkle's parodic performances draw attention to what the pornographer is trying to achieve with his (or hers). One thing the "pro-life" movement is doing is using exposures of fetuses to convince the public that two separate individuals exist in one body from the moment of conception. To draw attention to this aspect of their imagery, artists might create images that parody this view of human generation. How long does it take for one to equal two: an instant, a few days, or a few months?

To highlight the extent to which culture rather than nature plays a role in the onset of personhood, artists might borrow pop-cultural images of women's bodies rather than clinical or scientific-looking illustrations. For example, one very popular, unrealistic-looking icon of the feminine body is the Barbie doll. Although the promotion of Barbie's body has often been a source of oppression for women, recently some activists have appropriated the doll for subversive purposes. One recent book, *Barbie Unbound: A Parody of Barbie Obsession*,[105] features Barbie art to offer feminist lessons about sex, drugs, and HIV, among other things. A rash of guerrilla internet sites now advertise a variety of unorthodox Barbies, including "Pregnant Teen Barbie," "Back-Alley Abortion Barbie" (comes with coat hanger), and "Our Barbies Ourselves": "Anatomically correct Barbie both inside and out, comes with spreadable legs, her own speculum, magnifying glass, and detailed diagrams of female anatomy so that little girls can learn about their bodies in a friendly, non-threatening way. Also included . . . contraceptives, sex toys, expanding uterus with fetus at various stages of development . . . underscoring that each young woman has the right to choose what she does with her own Barbie."[106] "Our Barbies Ourselves" is a kind of "pro-choice" Barbie. To develop a "post-porn modernist" image of reproduction, we might try to transform "Our Barbie Ourselves" into "Post-Porn Reproductive Barbie."

Post-Porn Reproductive Barbie comes with a nondetachable Fetal Barbie inside her. To view Fetal Barbie, owners press the internal flashlight mechanism to make Fetal Barbie visible inside big Barbie's womb (figure 3.39). Another Post-Porn Barbie, Breeder Barbie, features the proverbial leaf-over-crotch image. The instructions read, "Pull back the leaf and you'll see that Barbie is *really* two Barbies, not one!" (figure 3.40). However, unlike the "pro-life" fetus, Fetal Barbie might fail to

Figure 3.39
L. Shrage, "Fetal Barbie," digital photomontage, 1999.

Figure 3.40
L. Shrage, "Breeder Barbie," digital photomontage, 1999.

pull back leaf and you have two Barbies instead of one!

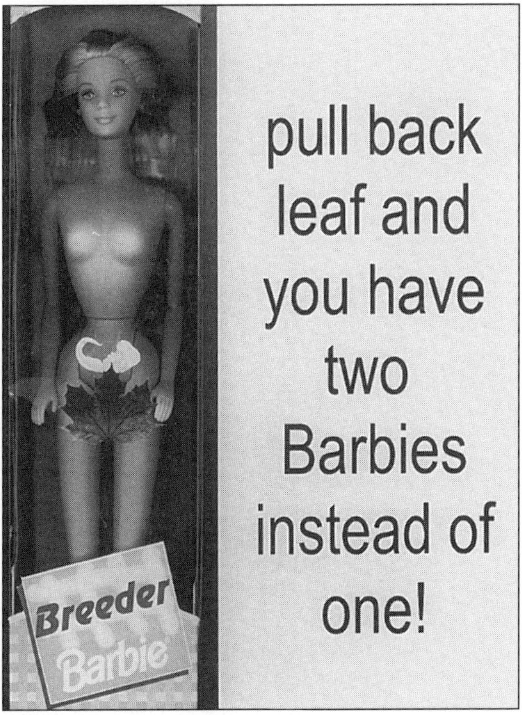

convince viewers that there is actually another tiny Barbie inside grownup Barbie (only a fool would pay more for this doll). Such images may encourage viewers to reflect on how the "pro-life" fetus is better groomed for sentimental value and stardom or, in other words, how the "pro-life" fetus is what Duden calls a "managed image."[107] We can also introduce Mass Media Barbie, who publicizes the medical risks of pregnancy and the need for reliable and affordable contraception (figure 3.41), or Ultrasound Barbie, who allows viewers to explore their perverse desire to see the normally unseen (figure 3.42).[108] The purpose of these images is to draw attention to the "pro-life" movement's intense interest in the fetus and their use of the mature fetus to promote infringements of women's privacy and inappropriate levels of compulsory service. By replacing the mature fetus with a younger one that resides in the body of a cultural icon, this postpornographic image aims to redirect the public's pornographic imaginations toward different ends. And because Fetal Barbie is less easy to personify than Barbie herself, these images of reproducing Barbies may challenge the idea that two separate dolls exist in one Barbie from the moment of conception.

Figure 3.41
L. Shrage, "Mass Media Barbie," digital photomontage, 1999.

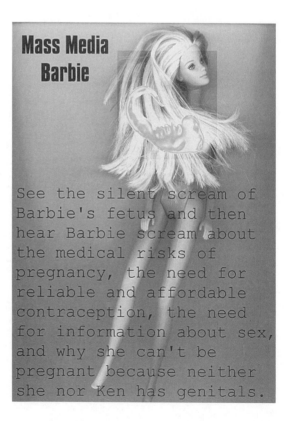

Mass Media Barbie

See the silent scream of Barbie's fetus and then hear Barbie scream about the medical risks of pregnancy, the need for reliable and affordable contraception, the need for information about sex, and why she can't be pregnant because neither she nor Ken has genitals.

Post-*porn* modernists might also consider appropriating the "managed fetus" for subversive purposes. Although this strange and fantastic image (to recall Hartouni) usually wears an antiabortion message, we can change its verbal garments. For instance, a poster might exploit the public's interest in fetuses to promote universal healthcare. The image and text would draw attention to the hypocrisy of many "pro-life" proponents who advocate state protection for fetuses while remaining indifferent to pregnant women who have no health insurance (figure 3.43). Such posters might be jarring and confusing. They seduce their audiences with the attractive and familiar fetus photos and then project an unexpected message—a progressive political proposal that will put the generally antiwelfare "pro-life" forces on the defensive. Another poster in this vein might parody the "pro-life" slogan "Abortion is child abuse," as well as their use of the phrase "unborn citizen," by conjoining the familiar fetus with a caption such as "Homelessness is citizen abuse." The prevalence of such images would serve to decouple the fetus from its antiabortion meanings, requiring viewers of this image to read for new meanings. In addition, "pro-life" fetuses could be incorporated in posters

Figure 3.42
L. Shrage, "Ultrasound Barbie," digital photomontage, 1999.

Figure 3.43
L. Shrage, "Life
Insurance," digital
photomontage, 1999.

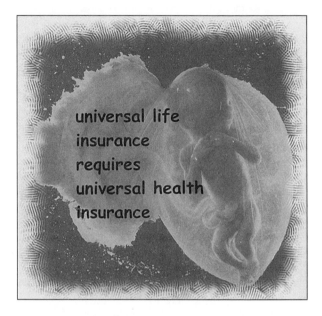

Figure 3.44
L. Shrage, digital
photomontage, 1999.

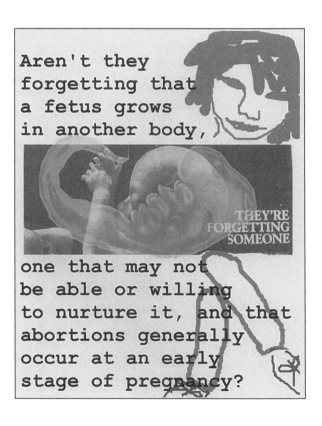

in ways that undermine the intended message of the original (figure 3.44). Or we might try parodies that place another image where viewers expect to find the fetus, to call attention to the fetus image as a social artifact (figures 3.45, 3.46).

Lynda Hart, who introduced the term "visibility politics," writes: "It is time perhaps to rethink Audre Lorde's mantra for feminist praxis: 'the master's tools will never dismantle the master's house.'"[109] In this

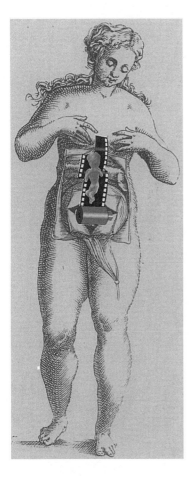

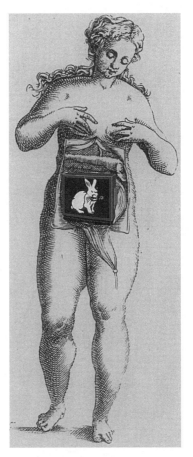

Figure 3.45
L. Shrage, digital photomontage, 1999.

Figure 3.46
L. Shrage, digital photomontage, 1999.

chapter, I am essentially encouraging feminists to take up our opponents' tools and fight back. This means, in part, moving feminist reproductive rights art out of journals and museums and into newspapers, bus terminals, the internet, film, and TV.[110] It also means developing a public campaign that addresses the important moral issues raised by abortion—the limits of our duties to others, the boundaries of privacy, how to balance respect for life with important human interests, and the social conditions that give women good choices. Past "pro-choice" campaigns have not addressed these issues well, but there is no shortage of feminist creativity to turn this situation around and to make sure that abortion rights defenders, and not the clinic-bombing fascists, have the good folk art in the future.

Conclusion
Abortion and Democracy

4

$\mathbf{A}$ decade ago, Ruth Bader Ginsburg claimed that "Roe . . . halted a political process that was moving in a reform direction and thereby, I believe, prolonged divisiveness and deferred stable settlement of the issue."[1] Ginsburg argues that the Court should have done no more than strike down the Texas law and should not have gone on to "fashion a regime blanketing the subject, a set of rules that displaced virtually every state law then in force."[2] Moreover, Ginsburg argues that

> the Roe decision might have been less of a storm center . . . had it both homed in more precisely on the women's equality dimension of the issue and, correspondingly, attempted nothing more bold at that time than the mode of decisionmaking the Court employed in the 1970s gender classification cases.[3]

In particular the Court could have acknowledged, as it did in 1992, "the intimate connection between a woman's 'ability to control her reproductive life' and her 'ability . . . to participate equally in the economic and social life of the Nation.'"[4] Although I agree with Ginsburg that *Roe*'s scheme was divisive and perpetuated the public abortion controversy, I have tried to show that a more moderate scheme could have been considerably less divisive. Moreover, a more moderate scheme is preferable to no scheme, in order to ensure that women have some period of access to unrestricted abortion. In chapter 1, I proposed that the time span for unrestricted abortion should correspond to the number of weeks most women need to arrange an abortion when there are no special circumstances involved. For many women, the safest contraceptive methods that they can use are not fail-proof, and thus women need some period of time to arrange abortions simply as back up birth control. Because controlling her fertility is essential for a woman's full participation in society, for maintaining her optimal health, and for controlling her personal destiny, there needs to be some period when a woman can request an abortion for any reason. Nevertheless the time span for nontherapeutic abortions can be considerably shorter than the period mandated by *Roe*.

In chapter 2, I argued that an equality defense, based on the equal right to be no more than a minimally decent Samaritan, provides justification for a more moderate scheme. This defense acknowledges that compulsory pregnancy, in many situations, imposes medical and socioeconomic burdens that go beyond what society commands from other potential aid-givers. This defense thus makes the connection between procreative autonomy and the conditions necessary for women's equal participation, as Ginsburg suggests. I have also argued that a compromise scheme could help build legislative momentum to remove barriers to abortion services and that legislative action is important, especially if funding restrictions on therapeutic and nontherapeutic abortions are not invalidated by the courts. But women's reproductive autonomy and equal participation depend on more than access to abortion, and I agree with those who argue that they depend on the existence of a minimally decent social and economic security net that enables women to choose parenting without risking destitution. I have argued that social expectations regarding pregnancy and abortion should take into consideration the forms of social assistance available to women and their families. When women do not have genuine access to abortion (e.g., because of their insurance status, lack of accessible providers, or inefficient judicial bypass procedures), or when bearing children imposes severe hardships that society chooses not to ameliorate, then restrictions on abortion need to be relaxed. Conversely, a society that wants to restrict abortion without discriminating against women, in order to advance important public interests, should provide various forms of social and economic assistance, such as universal health insurance, income support for poor families, and state-subsidized nursery and preschool programs.

A recent *Los Angeles Times* poll shows that support for *Roe* has slipped to 43 percent (in 2000) from 56 percent (in 1991).[5] This poll also shows that 65 percent of Americans oppose legal abortion in the second trimester, suggesting that the timing of an abortion is morally significant for many, as Annette Clark points out.[6] Analyzing the data in this poll and others, Clyde Wilcox and Julia Riches write: "Americans draw subtle distinctions on the abortion issue—about the reasons the woman seeks an abortion, about the gestational stage of the fetus, about the age and circumstances of the woman."[7] The public is sympathetic to the need for abortion when a woman's physical health is at risk and in cases of rape or incest or severe fetal defect. Support is considerably weaker for abortions to preserve a woman's mental or emotional health or for socioeconomic reasons such as poverty, too many children, marital status, and sex selection.[8] Although public opinion can be misguided, majorities hold sway in a democratic society unless their laws can be shown to violate a basic human or legal right. Activists should work to educate and inform public opinion, and there is certainly room to do so on abortion.

I have tried to show that the reasons for restricting abortion in the second trimester are not only strategic but are tied to general moral and political principles. These moral and political principles do not assume any particular religious perspective, and I have tried to avoid making controversial metaphysical assumptions about the fetus. Those who hold more extreme views on the fetus (e.g., that the fetus is a full person at conception or only an appendage of its mother's body until birth) will not be satisfied with my assumptions, but my aim has been to frame a position that will be acceptable to a more moderate group on both the metaphysical and political questions. I have also tried to frame a position that takes seriously the burdens of pregnancy and the unfairness of selecting women for forms of compulsory service that are not imposed on others.

I have argued that states should be permitted to prohibit nontherapeutic abortions earlier than viability. This assumes that the therapeutic exemptions permitted by law could be written in ways that make their intent reasonably clear. Many countries permit only therapeutic abortions, and in the United States, most states permit only therapeutic abortions after viability. But greater thought needs to be given to how such laws would be enforced. For example, how would women demonstrate that they meet the requirements for a therapeutic abortion, and how do we set limits on the personal information they would need to provide? Because there is significant value in allowing doctors to practice in accordance with their own best judgment, I would argue that the enforcement of therapeutic exemptions should defer to doctors' judgments. Adequate public oversight can be achieved by demanding internal professional regulation of abortion providers, for example, by having abortion decisions peer reviewed. Doctors who provided abortions in questionable cases could be subject to a variety of professional sanctions, with provisions for external judicial review and criminal sanctions in the most egregious cases. Some abortion rights proponents object that such systems of regulation give too much power to doctors, so that women who cannot afford to change doctors, or who live in parts of the country where there is hostility to abortion, may be at a disadvantage.[9] But to address this issue, we need not go as far as giving total decision-making power to a woman for six months. A compromise would be to devise procedures for women to appeal negative decisions, using hospital committees that included women's health advocates or a fair and efficient judicial bypass system. Although *Roe's* regulatory scheme diminished the authority of doctors over the abortion decision, it then handed control to affluent women, who can choose among increasingly scarce providers, and to state bureaucrats for the remainder of women.

The regulations I am proposing are not perfect, and they require much fine-tuning and experimentation. But these regulations would have both practical and symbolic value. Their practical value resides in their potential to generate greater public support for abortion policies and ultimately public support for removing barriers to early abortion that serve little public purpose and that discriminate against poor and young women. Their symbolic value resides in the extent to which they acknowledge the legitimate issues of people on different sides of this debate. I have tried to devise regulations that represent a compromise rather than a victory for one side. By reaching a compromise that seems reasonable to more people, we defuse hostilities and begin to open a more productive social dialogue. This dialogue may result in further challenges to abortion regulations down the road, as new technological possibilities and cultural understandings emerge. The important thing is that any compromise reflects a rigorous and inclusive public debate, and not the power of a particular religious or political group. With a compromise, no side gets everything it wants, which is part of the cost of living in a diverse and democratic society.

Some argue that the abortion issue opened up deep, preexisting differences between religious conservatives and secular liberals. I have tried to show that the depth of this controversy is partly a result of divisive policies. The regulatory scheme adopted by the Court in *Roe* so favored one side of the debate that those on the opposing side were forced into extreme opposition. Moderates who approve some abortions and not others were forced to choose between extremely restrictive or permissive policies, and eventually more complex positions have been obscured. Moreover, *Roe's* focus on women's interests, and relative neglect of the public interests at stake, divided opponents into advocates for the rights of fetuses and advocates for the rights of women—stances imagined as mutually exclusive. Had the rights of women been limited in a way that recognized the inherent worth of human life and our limited duties to help, the public would not have had to choose between absolute support for fetuses or for women. Instead, people holding a range of views on this issue could have endorsed conditional support for both.

Feminists are often struck by the creativity and persistence of abortion opponents and attribute their zeal to sinister motives. Yet the permissiveness of the *Roe* scheme, in relation to public opinion, created conditions for the cause of fetuses to be taken seriously. Although many abortion opponents are inspired by religious dogmas, some may simply be inspired by the injustice of destroying relatively developed human life without sufficient reason. As I tried to show in the previous chapter, those advocating the cause of fetuses are appropriating the political tools of social progressives to promote rights assumed to belong to fetuses. As avenues for political and legal reform close, those intent on ending the supposed injustices suffered by fetuses are carrying out subversive, anti–status quo, and sometimes successful, grassroots political organizing. Like previous groups that have fought for the rights of the oppressed, fetus advocates speak on behalf of the people they wish to liberate. That is, rather than seeing abortion as a struggle between public and private interests, the "pro-life" movement sees it as a struggle of the weak against the strong.

In the previous chapter I evaluated feminist debates about developing tactics to respond to fetus pictures. Yet these debates overlook another powerful tactic of abortion foes, which is to speak for the oppressed so that the latter's victimization is better understood by the public. Speaking for the oppressed is often necessary, because sometimes the oppressed cannot speak for themselves, and their stories therefore do not get heard. I am arguing that the strong sentiments and extreme tactics on behalf of fetuses are the result of controversial policies as much as of preexisting differences between those on the extreme ends of this controversy. If we understand these strong sentiments and extreme tactics as expressions of outrage, even if misguided, at unjust policies, rather than as expressions of misogynist religious ideologies, then we might be more inclined to see compromise as a reasonable strategy. "Pro-life" narratives that recover the voices of the oppressed suggest that those advocating on behalf of fetuses see themselves as advocates for social justice and not for their religious beliefs, even if others do not see them this way.

For example, in church basements and on college campuses and the internet, fetus rights advocates circulate narratives reminiscent of slave diaries. One is called "Diary of an Unborn Child" and relates the following tale.

> October 5—Today my life began. My parents do not know it yet, I am as small as a seed of an apple, but it is I already. And I am to be a girl. I shall have blond hair and blue eyes. Just about everything is settled though, even the fact that I shall love flowers.

> October 19—Some say I am not a real person yet, that only my mother exists. But I am a real person, just as a small crumb of bread is yet truly bread. My mother is. And I am.

> October 23—My mouth is just beginning to open now. Just think, in a year or so I shall be laughing and later talking. I know what my first word will be: MAMA.

> October 25—My heart began to beat today . . .

> November 12—Tiny fingers are beginning to form on my hands. Funny how small they are! I'll be able to stroke my mother's hair with them.

> November 20—It wasn't until today that the doctor told mom that I am living here under her heart. Oh, how happy she must be! Are you happy, mom?

> November 25—My mom and dad are probably thinking about a name for me . . .

> December 10—My hair is growing . . .

> December 13—I am just about able to see. It is dark around me. When mom brings me into the world it will be full of sunshine and flowers. But what I want more than anything is to see my mom . . .

> December 24—I wonder if mom hears the whispering of my heart? . . .

> December 28—Today my mother killed me.[10]

By narrating stories such as this, fetus advocates attempt to make us feel like repentant Nazis reading the *Diary of Anne Frank* or repentant racists reading the *Narrative of the Life of Frederick Douglass, An American Slave*. The flier containing this diary includes a "Chronology of the New Human Life," which offers a clinical and biological description of each stage of fetal life up to twenty weeks. We are told that "At 43 days, electrical brain wave patterns can be recorded. This is usually ample evidence that 'thinking' is taking place in the brain. The new life may be thought of as a thinking person." Although it is a huge leap to infer that the brain waves detected at forty-three days signify that thought is going on, especially thoughts anything like those recorded in "Diary of an Unborn," a similar mental leap may have once been necessary for white Jewish men to appreciate the rational abilities of Christian girls and black people. "First-person" fetus narratives are attempts to make us understand that fetuses are like us, in the ways we think and feel, and ultimately, to make us recognize the injustices of the practices allowed by *Roe*.

"Diary of an Unborn Child" is one of numerous imaginative efforts that attempt to give the "victims" of *Roe* a momentary spotlight. A song by Lauryn Hill, "To Zion," deploys another progressive political tool, which is to describe the transformation of participant in an oppressive system. Hill sings about the difficulty she had choosing not to have an abortion. Movingly, she sings:

> I knew his life deserved a chance / but everybody told me to be smart / "look at your career,"they said, / "Lauryn baby use your head." / But instead I chose to use my heart / Now the joy . . . of my world . . . / is in Zion! . . ./ Now the joy . . . of my world . . . / is in Zion! / How beautiful is nothing more / than to wait at Zion's door / I've never been in love like this before . . . / See I know that a gift so great / is only one God could create / And I'm reminded every time I see your face / that the joy . . . of my world . . . / is in Zion! / Now the joy . . . of my world . . . / is in Zion![11]

By using her heart instead of her head, the singer becomes a resister, a liberator. Had Hill chosen an abortion, she would have ended Zion's life. Zion would have been the victim of a heartless choice and policies that permit such choices. Such a choice about Zion is horrifying for a mother, and most listeners, to ponder.

Abortion opponents like to point out that any one of us might have been aborted, and they often suggest that legal abortion increases the chance that any existing person could have been the victim of this practice. Of course the chance that any existing person might not have existed is great, regardless of the legality of abortion. Our parents may never have met, our grandparents may never have met, our parents might have died as children, and so on. Should we regard the idea of someone never coming to be—of a world without a particular loved one—as a potential tragedy? Well, in some sense, yes, but if they never existed, of course we wouldn't. There is perhaps a paradox here. We see the possibility of someone we love having never existed as a tragic possibility. But if they really never existed, we would not experience their nonexistence as a tragedy. The song is moving because Zion exists and is a source of great joy, as are all children. Because he exists we can understand the possibility of a world without him as a tragic possibility. But if Zion had never come to be because of an abortion, neither we nor Hill would experience the loss in such tragic proportions.

"To Zion" conceives the fetus as a complete child and as "a gift only God can create." In "Diary of an Unborn Child" the fetus proclaims on the first day of its existence: "Just about everything is settled though, even the fact that I shall love flowers." This story assumes that biological conception results in a complete entity, with all its essential parts and traits, and that the rest of life is merely the expression of these genetically inscribed traits. These are controversial assumptions. Moreover, even if true, they wouldn't resolve the abortion issue, given that there are limits to the burdens we can be expected to assume for the sake of others. And some burdens are more costly than the interruption of a singer's career.

Both "Diary of an Unborn Child" and "To Zion," and the visual propaganda that feminists have studied, help sustain a political movement in which aborted fetuses are imagined as people who never made it into existence and in which people who made it are imagined as fetuses threatened with homicide. Fetuses who didn't make it are equated with the people who did, compelling activists to speak for those who have been silenced. I agree with Lauryn Hill that we need to open our hearts and not always let our intellects prevail. Opening our hearts might allow us to develop abortion policies that show compassion for women, for fetuses as they develop, for poor women, for young women, and for the disabled. Those who advocate for fetuses have overstated their case, but they have some legitimate issues that abortion policies can respect. These policies can also respect women's rights to great degree and avoid treating women differently on the basis of social class.

Notes

Chapter 1

1. In *Planned Parenthood of Southeastern Pennsylvania v. Casey* (1992), the Court replaced strict scrutiny with the "undue burden" test for state laws that potentially infringe a woman's right to abort. This weaker standard has been used to justify upholding numerous state laws that restrict access to abortion. See Lawrence H. Tribe, *Abortion: The Clash of Absolutes* (New York: Norton, 1992), 243–56. Regarding the impact of *Webster v. Reproductive Health Services* (1989), see Walter Dellinger and Gene Sperling, "Abortion and the Supreme Court: The Retreat from *Roe v. Wade*," *University of Pennsylvania Law Review* 138 (November 1989): 83–118.

2. *Planned Parenthood of Southeastern Pennsylvania v. Casey*, excerpted in *The Abortion Controversy*, ed. Eva R. Rubin (Westport, CT: Praeger, 1998), 263. Some of the factual assumptions that have changed over time are that abortions in the second trimester are now relatively safer because of new medical procedures and techniques and that viability is now thought to occur at 23–24 weeks rather than 28. Planned Parenthood Affiliates of California defines "viability" as "an 'anatomical threshold' when critical organs, such as the lungs and kidneys, can sustain independent life. Until the air sacs are mature enough to permit gases to pass into and out of the bloodstream, which is extremely unlikely until at least 23 weeks gestation (from last menstrual period), a fetus cannot be sustained even with a respirator, which can force air into the lungs but cannot pass gas from the lungs into the bloodstream." Planned Parenthood Affiliates of California, "Abortion and Fetal Viability" [online], May 1, 1997, available: http://www.ppacca.org/issues/read.asp?ID=44 (January 19, 2002).

3. 492 U.S. 490 (1989).

4. Sylvia Law, "Abortion Compromise—Inevitable but Impossible," *University of Illinois Law Review* (1992) (Lexis-Nexis document, obtained September 1, 2001).

5. U.N. Population Division, *Abortion Policies: A Global Review*, vol. 1 (New York: United Nations, 1992), 133. See also Center for Reproductive Law and Policy (CLRP), "The World's Abortion Laws 2000" (New York: CLRP, 2000), which is a map and chart summarizing statistical information pro-

vided by the Alan Guttmacher Institute. Most of this information is available online at: http://www.crlp.org/pri_worldlaws.html (January 20, 2002). A similar fact sheet, "World Abortion Policies 1999," is available from the U.N. Population Division, Department of Economic and Social Affairs, United Nations, New York, NY 10017.

6. U.N. Population Division, *Abortion Policies*, vol. 1, 106.

7. U.N. Population Division, *Abortion Policies*, vol. 2 (New York: United Nations, 1993), 58.

8. Ibid., 75.

9. Ibid., 32.

10. Ibid.,180.

11. U.N. Population Division, *Abortion Policies*, vol. 3 (New York: United Nations, 1995), 114.

12. Ibid., 141.

13. Before ten weeks of gestation, "menstrual regulation" is employed. What this means is that a woman can have a procedure performed to remove the contents of her uterus (with vacuum aspiration or drugs) without first having to undergo a test to confirm the existence of a pregnancy. *Abortion Policies*, vol. 1, 98.

14. *Abortion Policies*, vol. 3, 138.

15. Abortion Law Reform Association (ALRA), "The Campaign for Choice" [online], available: http://www.alra.org.uk/whychan.html (January 19, 2002). Also see *Abortion Policies*, vol. 3, 155–57.

16. Mary Ann Glendon, *Abortion and Divorce in Western Law*, (Cambridge: Harvard University Press, 1987), 24.

17. Ibid., 22. Emphasis in original.

18. *Abortion Policies*, vol. 1, 85. See also Glendon, *Abortion and Divorce in Western Law*, 24.

19. See Mark Tushnet, *Abortion*, Constitutional Issues Series (New York: Facts on File, 1996), 82, and 76–78.

20. Donald P. Kommers, "Abortion and the Constitution: The Cases of the United States and West Germany," in *Abortion: New Directions for Policy Studies*, ed. Edward Manier, William Lu, and David Solomon (Notre Dame, IN: University of Notre Dame Press, 1977), 109.

21. See note 2.

22. Alan Zaitchik, "Viability and the Morality of Abortion," in *The Problem of Abortion*, 2nd ed., ed. Joel Feinberg (Belmont, CA: Wadsworth, 1984), 60–1.

23. *Roe* stipulates that, after viability, the state may not prohibit abortion when it is "necessary, in appropriate medical judgment, for the preservation of the life or health of the mother." Moreover *Roe* permits, but does not require, states to prohibit abortion after viability. These stipulations deprive the fetus of due process and equal protection of the laws, which under the Fourteenth Amendment is granted to persons. See Roger Wertheimer, "Understanding Blackmun's Argument," in *Abortion: Moral and Legal Perspectives*, ed. Jay L. Garfield and Patricia Hennessey (Amherst: University of Massachusetts Press, 1984), 107. See also Ronald

Dworkin, *Life's Dominion: An Argument about Abortion, Euthanasia, and Individual Freedom* (New York: Knopf, 1993), 110–11.

24. Wertheimer, "Understanding Blackmun's Argument," 120. On the arbitrariness of viability as the point when the state's interest in potential life becomes compelling, see also Robert Blank, "Judicial Decision Making and Biological Fact: *Roe v. Wade* and the Unresolved Question of Fetal Viability," *Western Political Quarterly* 37 (1984), 588–89.

25. Nancy K. Rhoden, "The New Neonatal Dilemma: Live Births from Late Abortions," *Georgetown Law Journal* 72 (June 1984), 25 (all page references are to a Lexis-Nexis document, obtained July 2001).

26. Blank, "Judicial Decision Making and Biological Fact," 586. Also see Mathieu Deflem, "The Boundaries of Abortion Law: Systems Theories from Parsons to Luhmann and Habermas," *Social Forces* 76 (1998): 775–818; also available: www.sla.purdue.edu/people/soc/mdeflem/zaborsf.htm. For a discussion of the appropriate relationship between science and law with respect to viability, see Nancy K. Rhoden, "Trimesters and Technology: Revamping *Roe v. Wade*," *Yale Law Journal* 95 (March 1986): 691–97. Janet Brodie writes that "For two centuries in America, abortion had been treated according to common law tradition in which abortions before 'quickening'—fetal movement—were not punishable, and those procured later, after quickening, might be high misdemeanors if the woman died, but not felonies." 'Quickening' is understood by some to be the moment in a pregnancy when the child gives some sign of life (e.g., by moving), presumably because the soul has entered the body. In the 1830s and 1840s, some states criminalized abortion and Brodie writes that seven state supreme courts between 1840 and 1860 "upheld the common law tradition and ruled that an abortion before quickening was not a criminal offense." By invoking 'viability' in 1973, the Supreme Court managed to avoid the religious connotations of 'quickening,' and perhaps 'viability' should be viewed as the twentieth century substitute for 'quickening.' See Janet Farrell Brodie, *Conception and Abortion in Nineteenth-Century America* (Ithaca: Cornell University Press, 1994), 254.

27. David Garrow, *Liberty and Sexuality* (New York: Macmillan, 1994), 580–81.

28. *Roe v. Wade*, 410 U.S. 113 (1973), note 40.

29. See David Garrow, "From Reform to Repeal: The *Right* to Abortion, 1967–1969," in *Liberty and Sexuality*, 335–89. Also see Tushnet, *Abortion*, 46–58; and Tribe, *Abortion*, 43–49.

30. *Roe v. Wade*, note 41.

31. See PBS Online NewsHour Online Forums, http://www.pbs.org/newshour/forum/january98/roe2.html.

32. Garrow, *Liberty and Sexuality*, 583.

33. David Garrow, "Revelations on the Road to *Roe*," *American Lawyer* (May 2000): 83.

34. *Janice Abele et al. v. Arnold Markle et al.*, 351 F. Supp. 224 (Conn. September 20, 1972).

35. Ibid. A number of years after *Roe*, Ellen Frankel Paul and Jeffrey Paul

took up the "live birth" problem. They argued that, while the woman's ownership of her body justifies her right to abort, a fetus capable of independent existence owns its body, and thus a woman's right of bodily control does not give her the right to intentionally kill a fetus who happens to survive an abortion. Ellen Frankel Paul and Jeffrey Paul, "Self-ownership, Abortion and Infanticide," *Journal of Medical Ethics* 5 (1979): 133–38.

36. *Abele v. Markle*, 351 F. Supp. 224 (Conn. September 20, 1972).

37. Ibid.

38. According to Mark Tushnet, a letter to Blackmun from Marshall "suggested modifying Blackmun's general approach: Instead of barring state regulations before the first trimester and allowing extensive regulation after that, the opinion should allow state regulations 'directed at health and safety alone' between the end of the first trimester and viability. Brennan then sent a letter bolstering Marshall's suggestion. Blackmun immediately decided to accept the new approach, and as Powell's biographer puts it, 'Marshall's compromise became law.'" Mark Tushnet, *Making Constitutional Law: Thurgood Marshall and the Supreme Court, 1961–1991* (New York: Oxford University Press, 1997), 7.

39. David Garrow, "Revelations on the Road to *Roe*," 83.

40. Ibid., 83.

41. On the need for judicial restraint, see Cass Sunstein, *Legal Reasoning and Political Conflict* (New York: Oxford University Press, 1996), 175–78.

42. Garrow, *Liberty and Sexuality*, 582.

43. Ibid., 583–84.

44. Tushnet, *Making Constitutional Law*, 7.

45. Garrow, "Revelations on the Road to *Roe*," 83.

46. From their book *The Brethren*, excerpted in Rubin, *The Abortion Controversy*, 129.

47. A memo from Powell to Blackmun says: "the women who most need the benefit of liberalized abortion laws are likely to be young, inexperienced, unsure, frightened and perhaps unmarried . . . if there is a constitutional right to an abortion, there is much to be said for making it effective where and when it may well be needed most." Garrow notes that Powell never sent this memo and speculates that it may be because he discussed the contents with Blackmun in person, or he felt the points had been made well enough by others. Garrow, "Revelations on the Road to *Roe*," 83. Interestingly, Powell later decided with the majority of the Court that it was constitutional for states to refuse to pay for elective abortions for poor women. According to Rickie Solinger, "When the Supreme Court decided that the state of Connecticut could refuse to pay for a poor woman's elective abortion, the Court emphasized that lack of money could indeed prevent a woman from getting an abortion. Justice Lewis Powell explained for the majority, however, that the Connecticut abortion funding regulation didn't cause that woman's poverty. And the state regulation itself didn't stop the woman from obtaining an abortion. Powell wrote that the Court was sympathetic to the plight of the poor woman

who wants an abortion but doesn't have the money to pay for it. But for the Court's majority, Powell explained, the main point was 'the Constitution does not provide judicial remedies for every social and economic ill.'" See Rickie Solinger, *Beggars and Choosers: How the Politics of Choice Shapes Adoption, Abortion, and Welfare in the United States* (New York: Hill and Wang, 2001), 16–17. The case Solinger is discussing is *Maher v. Roe*, 432 USW 500. Brennan, Marshall, and Blackmun wrote in their dissent that restricting funding showed a "distressing insensitivity to the plight of impoverished women." Quoted in Solinger, *Beggars and Choosers*, p. 14. Evidently, though Powell was instrumental in increasing the time women had to arrange nontherapeutic abortions, he was perhaps less sensitive to the plight of poor women than some of his colleagues. Moreover, he evidently held that the state should not too severely restrict the time a woman has to obtain an abortion but it could severely restrict the use of public funds. By contrast, according to Michael Davis and Hunter Clark, Marshall "accused the majority [in *Beal v. Doe*] of pulling 'from thin air a distinction between laws that absolutely prevent exercise of the fundamental right to abortion and those that 'merely' make its exercise difficult for some people.'" See Michael D. Davis and Hunter R. Clark, *Thurgood Marshall: Warrior at the Bar, Rebel on the Bench* (New York: Birch Lane Press, 1992), 343–44. In chapter 2, I discuss the relationship between the privacy defense and funding.

48. Rubin, *The Abortion Controversy*, 129–30.
49. Zaitchik, "Viability and the Morality of Abortion," 59–60.
50. Of course, if the state decided to fund high-quality neonatal care for the premature infants of the rural poor, but not contraception and abortion, then the fetuses of these women would be "viable" earlier, thus shortening their time to arrange abortions. Now that we've seen, post-*Roe*, how effectively funding can be used to limit abortion, such a possibility does not seem at all unlikely.
51. Wertheimer, "Understanding Blackmun's Argument," 120.
52. For a relatively recent version of this criticism, see Jeffrey Reiman, *Abortion and the Ways We Value Human Life* (Lanham, MD: Rowman and Littlefield, 1999), 53–54.
53. Rhoden, "Trimesters and Technology," 660. Regarding the practical difficulties in estimating fetal viability, see also Carole Clark, "Perspectives of Viability," *Arizona State Law Journal* [12] (1980): 130–33.
54. *Abele v. Markle*, 351 F. Supp. 224 (Conn. September 20, 1972)
55. Heather Gert, "Viability," in *The Problem of Abortion*, 3rd ed., ed. Joel Feinberg (Belmont, CA: Wadsworth, 1997), 121.
56. Ibid., 124.
57. *Abele v. Markle*, 351 F. Supp. 224 (Conn. September 20, 1972).
58. Rhoden, "The New Neonatal Dilemma," 7-9; "Trimesters and Technology," 664–65.
59. "Preterm birth, which occurs in about 10 percent of all pregnancies, is associated with 75 percent of all infant deaths, and, by age 2, one-fifth to one-third of preterm children suffer from moderate to severe sensory

handicaps, including such disabilities as cerebral palsy, mental retardation, epilepsy, blindness and deafness, Sandman [Professor of Psychiatry and Human Behavior at UC Irvine] said. The economic consequences of prematurity are of a magnitude similar to smoking, alcohol abuse and AIDS. As much as 35 percent ($4 billion) of the $11.4 billion spent annually on infant health care in the United States is for costs related to prematurity, and the cost of a stay in neonatal intensive care for a preterm infant ranges from $20,000–$140,000, he added." "Study Led by UC Irvine Researcher to Explore Role of Stress in Premature Births" [online], October 14, 1998, available at University of California, Irvine Medical Center/Medical Group: http://www.ucihealth.com/News/Releases/101498st.htm (August 2001); Nancy Rhoden criticizes a similar proposal by John Robertson in "The New Neonatal Dilemma," 26.

60. Rhoden, "Trimesters and Technology," 655–66.

61. Ibid.

62. Tushnet writes that "Justice Harry Blackmun had served as general counsel to the Mayo Clinic in Rochester, Minnesota, before he was appointed to the federal bench. He was particularly sensitive to the impact of restrictive abortion laws on doctors who sometimes felt a conflict between the law's demands and their own medical judgment." Tushnet, *Abortion*, 64.

63. Gert, "Viability," 121.

64. Garrow, *Liberty and Sexuality*, 377, 382, 411, 479–80, and 489–90. See also Tushnet, *Abortion*, 53.

65. Garrow, "Revelations on the Road to *Roe*," 83. As I mentioned in note 47, Garrow informs us that Powell never sent this memo to Blackmun, though Garrow suggests that it may be because Powell or the other justices discussed these issues with Blackmun in person. See also p. 147, note 2.

66. Ibid., 82.

67. Tribe, "Structural Due Process," Harvard Civil Rights–Civil Liberties Law Review 10, 2 (spring 1975): 269–321, quoted in Joan Hoff, *Law, Gender, and Injustice: A Legal History of U.S. Women* (New York: New York University Press, 1991), 308. Hoff restates Tribe's point in the following way: "the definition of viability in *Roe*, far from reflecting arbitrary judicial preference, theoretically allowed for considerable flexibility. It could have permitted each generation, depending upon advances in medical technology, to determine when the 'fetus may become viable'" (308). According to Hoff, Tribe has retreated from this position.

68. Alexander Bickel, *The Morality of Consent* (New Haven: Yale University Press, 1975), 27.

69. Sunstein, *Legal Reasoning and Political Conflict*, 180–81.

70. See Marlene Gerber Fried, "Abortion in the United States: Legal but Inaccessible," in *Abortion Wars: A Half Century of Struggle, 1950–2000*, ed. Rickie Solinger (Berkeley: University of California Press, 1998), 210–11.

71. Rhoden, "Trimesters and Technology," 666.

72. Rhoden points out that in *Colautti v. Franklin,* and *Planned Parenthood v. Danforth,* the courts have upheld the principle that a woman has a right to use the abortion procedure that is safest for her. Ibid., 679, note 191.
73. *Stenberg v. Carhart,* see *New York Times,* June 29, 2000, 20.
74. See Rhoden, "Trimesters and Technology," 680, and 679, note 192. Rhoden writes that abortion is now safer than childbirth even after week 21. Viability is thought to occur now around 22 or 23 weeks.
75. In *Akron v. Akron Center for Reproductive Health,* 462 U.S. 416 (1983).
76. Rhoden, "Trimesters and Technology," 675.
77. Rhoden makes a similar point using the analogy of a 55 mph speed limit, ibid., 677.
78. Ibid., 671–72.
79. Some schemes have graduated cutoffs, so that abortions for mental health or socioeconomic reasons are permitted after an initial period of unrestricted abortion but only up to twenty weeks, while abortions for physical health reasons are permitted beyond twenty weeks. See, Center for Reproductive Law and Policy, "The World's Abortion Laws 2000."
80. Judith Blake, "The Abortion Decisions: Judicial Review and Public Opinion," in Manier, Lu, and Solomon, *Abortion,* 55.
81. See ibid., 51–82; and Everett Carll Ladd and Karlyn H. Bowman, *Public Opinion about Abortion: Twenty-five Years after Roe v. Wade* (Washington, DC: American Enterprise Institute Press, 1997), 9.
82. See note 1.
83. In her "Chronology of Abortion Politics," Rickie Solinger writes that by 1992, "eighty-four percent of counties in [the] United States have no physician willing to perform abortions." In Solinger, *Abortion Wars,* xiv. Judith Boss mentions "the reluctance of younger doctors to provide abortions (two-thirds of abortion providers are now over the age of sixty-five). . . . In 1995 only 33 percent of obstetrician-gynecologists, compared with 42 percent in 1983, were performing abortions." See Judith Boss, *Analyzing Moral Issues,* 2nd ed. (Boston: McGraw-Hill, 2002), 103.
84. See Ana Teresa Ortiz, "'Bare-Handed' Medicine and Its Elusive Patients: The Unstable Construction of Pregnant Women and Fetuses in Dominican Obstetrics Discourse," *Feminist Studies* 23 (summer 1997): 263–88.
85. Kristin Luker, *Abortion and the Politics of Motherhood* (Berkeley: University of California Press, 1984), 237.
86. The AMA scheme is discussed in *Roe.*
87. Dworkin, *Life's Dominion,* 171.
88. Ibid., 169.
89. Ibid., 169.
90. Ibid., 157.
91. Dworkin may prefer "sentience" for the same reasons Blackmun preferred "viability," in that it seems to offer a neutral, scientific way to determine when the fetus has interests. Yet whether we adopt an apparently scientific indicator of the fetus's abilities and interests or a spiritual one depends on our religious or secular orientation to the world.
92. Ibid., 170.

93. "Nearly two-thirds of respondents say abortions should be illegal after the first three months of pregnancy" in a recent national poll. See Alissa J. Rubin, "Americans Narrowing Support for Abortions," *Los Angeles Times* [online], June 18, 2000, available: http://www.latimes.com/news/custom/timespoll/la-000618abortpoll.story (January 21, 2002)
94. Dworkin, *Life's Dominion*, 13.
95. Ibid., 101.
96. Glendon, *Abortion and Divorce in Western Law*, 39.
97. Kommers, "Abortion and the Constitution," 96–98. Since unification, Germany's abortion laws have been revised to work out the policy differences that existed between the two German states. This seems to have led to policies that decriminalize abortion in the first trimester, but require mandatory patient counseling to communicate the prima facie wrongness of an abortion and the value of the fetus's life. A 1992 parliamentary act recognized that "the State's duty to protect developing life could be better served, in general, by improving the social environment for women and families with children . . . than by threatening punishment." Susanne Walther, quoted in Donald P. Kommers, *The Constitutional Jurisprudence of the Federal Republic of Germany*, 2nd ed. (Durham, NC: Duke University Press, 1997), 348.
98. Welfare policies with income allowances that are grossly inadequate to meet a family's minimum food and shelter requirements, that deny benefits to children conceived while their mothers were on welfare, and that fail to provide adequate childcare programs or allowances for poor working parents are the kind of policies I have in mind. For a recent article on how these policies encourage abortion, see Karen Houppert, "For Her Own Good," *The Nation*, February 4, 2002, 20–24.
99. Ruth Colker, *Abortion and Dialogue* (Bloomington: Indiana University Press, 1992), 125. Alison Jaggar similarly views the regulation of abortion and reproduction as contingent on a society's social security provisions in Jaggar, "Abortion and a Woman's Right to Decide," in *Women and Philosophy: Toward a Theory of Liberation*, ed. Carol Gould and Marx Wartofsky (New York: Capricorn Books, 1976), 347–60.
100. Colker, *Abortion and Dialogue*, 118. Ronald Dworkin objects to Glendon's view for some of the same reasons as Colker, see Dworkin, *Life's Dominion*, 62.
101. Glendon, *Abortion and Divorce in Western Law*, 53. Many states now have laws that shift some economic responsibility for children onto their biological fathers (or to the parents of men who are minors). Yet policies that do this will not take the place of adequate welfare policies, for many such men will be hard to locate, poor, or simply unwilling to assume responsibility, even with significant social pressure. And while the government can make efforts to establish paternity and collect child support, some efforts will be counterproductive and not in the child's best interest, for example if the father has a history of violent and abusive behavior. Thus, while such policies are not bad, they represent only a small, essentially individualist, step.

102. Sunstein, *Legal Reasoning and Political Conflict*, 176.
103. Dorothy Roberts, *Killing the Black Body: Race, Reproduction and the Meaning of Liberty* (New York: Pantheon Books, 1997), 300.
104. Ibid., 300.
105. Rickie Solinger, *Beggars and Choosers*, 7.
106. Andrea Press and Elizabeth Cole, *Speaking of Abortion: Television and Authority in the Lives of Women* (Chicago: University of Chicago Press, 1999), 27, 26–32.

Chapter 2

1. Anita Allen, "Privacy and Equal Protection as Bases for Abortion Law," in *Having and Raising Children: Unconventional Families, Hard Choices, and the Social Good*, ed. Uma Narayan and Julia J. Bartkowiak (University Park: Pennsylvania State University Press, 1999), 134.
2. Mark Tushnet, *Abortion*, Constitutional Issues Series (New York: Facts on File, 1996), 71. In a memo Brennan wrote to Blackmun on December 13, 1972, he writes:

> I too welcome your giving second thoughts to the choice of the end of the first trimester as the point beyond which a state may appropriately regulate abortion practices. But if the "cut-off" point is to be moved forward somewhat, I am not sure that the point of "viability" is the appropriate point, at least in a technical sense. I read your proposed opinions as saying, and I agree, that a woman's right of personal privacy includes the abortion decision, subject only to limited regulation necessitated by the compelling state interests you identify. Moreover, I read the opinions to say that the state's initial interests . . . are in safeguarding the health of the woman and in maintaining medical standards. If this be the case, is the choice of "viability" as the point where a state may begin to regulate abortions appropriate? For if we identify the state's initial interests as the health of the woman and the maintenance of medical standards, the selection of "viability" (i.e., the point in time where the fetus is capable of living outside of the woman) as the point where a state may begin to regulate in consequence of these interests seems to me to be technically inconsistent.
>
> "Viability," I have thought, is a concept that focuses upon the fetus rather than the woman . . .

Brennan goes on to suggest that the cutoff point after which states may regulate should be couched neither in terms of trimesters, weeks, nor "viability," but rather "at the point in time where abortions become medically more complex." Brennan recommends allowing medically informed state legislatures to decide when this point occurs, but suggests that it would be "somewhere between 16 to 24 weeks" or the stage when a D & C was not possible and induced labor or Caesarean section would be used instead. He then writes "Then we might go on to say that at some later stage of pregnancy (i.e., after the fetus becomes 'viable') the state may well have an interest in protecting the potential life of the child and therefore a different and possibly broader scheme of state regulation would become permissible." What this memo shows is that Brennan objected to having a single cutoff point couched in terms of "viability." Though Powell argued that the viability time span for nontherapeutic abortion was more consistent with the privacy rationale, Brennan pointed out that a cutoff defined in terms of fetal viability was technically inconsistent with the state's reasons for invading a woman's privacy. Blackmun's final draft of *Roe* adopted a dual-cutoff scheme (which Brennan tacitly supports in this memo), but Blackmun unfortunately did couch the first cutoff in terms of the "first trimester" which has subsequently been criticized for being too rigid and not medically accurate. However, the language Brennan preferred, "at the point in time where abortions become medically more complex," would probably not permit states today to regulate abortions "between 16 and 24" weeks or even somewhat after that, as now D & C can be performed much later in pregnancy. I am very grateful to Jane DeHart, who provided me with a copy of this memo.

3. For a helpful discussion of the ways that the right to abort has become a class right, see Rickie Solinger, *Beggars and Choosers: How the Politics of Choice Shapes Adoption, Abortion, and Welfare in the United States* (New York: Hill and Wang, 2001), 12–20.

4. Cass Sunstein, "Neutrality in Constitutional Law (with Special Reference to Pornography, Abortion, and Surrogacy)," *Columbia Law Review* 92 (January 1992): 30–31.

5. Allen, "Privacy and Equal Protection as Bases for Abortion Law," 129.

6. Ibid., 128.

7. Ibid., 134.

8. Jeremy Waldron, "Homelessness and the Issue of Freedom," in *Contemporary Political Theory*, ed. Robert Goodin and Philip Pettit (Oxford: Blackwell, 1997), 446–62.

9. Some feminist lawyers are challenging, on equal protection grounds, both private and public health insurers who provide coverage for Viagra for men but deny coverage for contraception and abortion for women. Yet so far, these suits are demanding coverage for therapeutic abortions—abortions approved by a doctor to preserve a woman's health—not nontherapeutic abortions. Thus even if these suits succeed, women will not be entitled to Medicaid coverage for nontherapeutic abortions. See the Center for Reproductive Law and Policy's recent coverage of one of these cases [online], available: http://www.crlp.org/pr_01_0712FLmedicaid.html (December 5, 2001).

10. Donald H. Regan, "Rewriting *Roe v. Wade*," *Michigan Law Review* 77 (August 1979): 1569.

11. Ibid., 1593–98.

12. Ibid., 1598–1600.

13. Ibid., 1601–2.

14. Regan refers to the "bad-samaritan principle" (ibid., 1573–1578, 1601), a

phrase that suggests that we have a right to be "bad Samaritans." Regan credits Judith Thomson's "A Defense of Abortion" for the idea of the pregnant woman as Samaritan (note 4, 1576). In this article, Thomson argues for the right to be only minimally decent Samaritans and against the obligation to be good Samaritans rather than the right to be indecent or bad Samaritans. I think this is a more plausible position, and thus I avoid talking in terms of the permission or right to be bad Samaritans. I discuss Thomson's "minimally decent" standard further on.

15. Ibid., 1569–70, 1589, 1596, 1600, 1609, and 1621–29.
16. Ibid., 1620.
17. Ibid., 1606.
18. Ibid., 1607.
19. Cass Sunstein, "Neutrality in Constitutional Law," 36.
20. For an interesting article regarding the possibility of male pregnancy using embryo transfer, see Dick Teresi and Kathleen McAuliffe, "Male Pregnancy," in *Sex/Machine: Readings in Culture, Gender, and Technology*, ed. Patrick D. Hopkins (Bloomington: Indiana University Press, 1998), 175–183.
21. Georgia Warnke makes a similar point. She writes "it remains unclear on Sunstein's analysis why antiabortion advocates could not push the demand for equality in a direction opposite to the one he imagines. Why might they not simply insist for the sake of consistency that the state impose 'good Samaritan' and duty-to-rescue laws on men as well as women? . . . If the problem with laws restricting or preventing abortion is that they impose caretaking functions on women that they do not impose on men, then it seems that the requirements for a more coherent understanding of equality could be met by imposing these functions on men as well. Georgia Warnke, *Legitimate Differences: Interpretation in the Abortion Controversy and Other Public Debates* (Berkeley: University of California Press, 1999), 105.
22. Regan, *"Rewriting Roe v. Wade,"* 1631.
23. Ibid., 1642.
24. Ibid., 1642.
25. Ibid., 1643. Linda McClain similarly argues that duties to rescue do not justify proscribing abortion before viability. She writes that "The Supreme Court adopted viability as a principled point before which abortion cannot be prohibited precisely because prior to that time, only the pregnant woman can sustain the fetus." McClain argues that prohibiting abortion prior to viability would place a special burden on women because, before viability, each fetus depends on a particular woman's body, whereas after viability it can theoretically survive without depending on a particular woman's body. However, if the fetus, after viability, does not depend on a particular woman's body, why would the court choose that moment to force a woman to continue to support a fetus with her body? This is the puzzle about viability that Heather Gert raises—a puzzle that Nancy Rhoden's work on viability and the live birth problem illuminates, which I discussed in chapter 1. See section V, C. 3. in Linda C. McClain,

"'Atomistic Man' Revisited: Liberalism, Connection, and Feminist Jurisprudence," *Southern California Law Review* 65 (March 1992) (Lexis-Nexis document, obtained March 2002).

26. Regan, "Rewriting *Roe v. Wade*" note 117, 1643. Emphasis in original.
27. Ibid., note 116, 1643.
28. This assumes, of course, that it is feasible for women to arrange abortions that meet such restrictions. If so, then the restrictions would serve the purpose of discouraging women from delaying abortions. In chapter 1, I argued that access to abortion for many women depends not only on how much time they have but also on the cost of abortion services, their insurance status, the proximity of providers, the bureaucratic approvals needed, educational outreach to young women, and so on. If many unnecessary social, economic, and informational obstacles were removed, it would be feasible for women to arrange nontherapeutic abortions significantly earlier than six months.
29. The act of killing imposed on those who must perform the surgery is also, I would imagine, qualitatively worse, which may be partly responsible for the scarcity of providers for late nontherapeutic abortions. However, as long as the provision of nontherapeutic abortion services is voluntary, I don't think we need to restrict abortion on behalf of providers.
30. Jeff McMahan, "The Right to Choose an Abortion," *Philosophy and Public Affairs* 22 (fall 1993): 335.
31. If the lack of access to abortion services were to count as a good enough reason (due to the lack of income, one's insurance status, the scarcity of providers, etc.), then society would need to create programs that ensure access to early abortion services if it wants to decrease the number of late abortions.
32. Regan, "Rewriting *Roe v. Wade*," 1583–84.
33. Ibid., 1585.
34. Judith Jarvis Thomson, "A Defense of Abortion," in Feinberg, *The Problem of Abortion*, 185. See note 14.
35. Ibid., 186–87.
36. Meredith Michaels, "Abortion and the Claims of Samaritanism," in *Abortion: Moral and Legal Perspectives*, ed. Jay Garfield and Patricia Hennessey (Amherst: University of Massachusetts Press, 1984), 213–26.
37. F. M. Kamm, *Creation and Abortion: A Study in Moral and Legal Philosophy* (New York: Oxford University Press, 1992), 209. Margaret Little also explores the question of the level of support a parent owes to a child and suggests that it depends on "a lived emotional interconnection, and a history of shared experiences" rather than mere genetic relatedness. She argues that there are times when it is legitimate for a person not to pursue a deeper relationship with a biological relative or offspring, and that a genetic connection between offspring and parent is the basis of "thin parenthood" rather than "thick parenthood." Thin parenthood might obligate one to be open to pursuing a deeper relationship, whereas thick parenthood involves a personal relationship and raises obligations of support. Whether a woman has a thin or thick relationship with her fetus seems to

depend, for Little, on how the woman conceives and experiences her relationship with it. I agree with Little that genetic relatedness is not sufficient to render a woman a parent in the "thick" sense, and I think a woman's conception of her relationship with a fetus is relevant to whether she has entered "thick" or only "thin" parenthood. But I also think the time she remains pregnant and whether she makes any efforts to end her pregnancy are also relevant. In other words, a woman's relationship to her fetus becomes thicker the longer she voluntarily or passively endures a pregnancy. Yet, there still need to be some limits on the forms of support thick parents owe to their children. See Margaret Olivia Little, "Abortion, Intimacy, and the Duty to Gestate," *Ethical Theory and Moral Practice* 2 (1999): 305–12.

38. Kamm, *Creation and Abortion,* 36.

39. Ibid., 95.

40. McMahan, "The Right to Choose an Abortion, 346–47. Kamm and Regan both hold that a woman's obligation to provide aid to a fetus is contingent on her having committed an action that makes the fetus worse off than it otherwise would have been, rather than on her committing an action that causes someone to need her help to avoid injury or death. McMahan's is a weaker standard, and one that I find somewhat plausible. Suppose Dr. Frankenstein succeeds in bringing a corpse to life, and suppose this human creature is now dependent on Dr. Frankenstein's scientific knowledge to maintain its life. Dr. Frankenstein's action of bringing the human creature to life did not make a person worse off than he would have been otherwise, but his action has caused someone to be dependent on him to avoid serious injury or death. Ann Garry discusses various concepts of responsibility that apply to pregnancy in "Abortion: Models of Responsibility," *Law and Philosophy* 2 (1983): 371–96.

41. Should abortion opponents ever be successful in establishing legally that a fetus is a person from conception onward, it is important for abortion rights proponents to have arguments that show that some abortions are acceptable, even if the fetus is a person. See also McMahan, 348.

42. Regan, "Rewriting *Roe v. Wade,*" 1611. Regan acknowledges that the right-to-refuse-to-help defense will not satisfy critics who see abortion as deliberate killing, and he discusses the self-defense argument.

43. See ibid., 1613–16.

44. Nancy Davis, "Abortion and Self Defense," in Garfield and Hennessey, *Abortion,* 193–94. Davis criticizes Regan, who assumes that, if the woman has a right to kill her fetus to defend herself, a physician has the right to assist her.

45. Eileen McDonagh, *Breaking the Abortion Deadlock: From Choice to Consent* (New York: Oxford University Press, 1996), 105, 152–53, and 174.

46. Ibid., 145.

47. Ibid., 151–52.

48. Ibid., 172.

49. Robin West argues that McDonagh has shown that women have a moral and political right (in a liberal state) to state protection against unwanted

pregnancy, and she agrees that women ought to have a constitutional right to this assistance, but she argues that relevant Supreme Court precedents have substantially weakened our constitutional rights to protection from private assaults. Robin West, "Liberalism and Abortion," *Georgetown Law Review* 87, 6 (June 1999): 2132–37.

50. McDonagh, *Breaking the Abortion Deadlock*, 36–37. Robin West also comments on this aspect of McDonagh's view in "Liberalism and Abortion," 2118.

51. McDonagh, *Breaking the Abortion Deadlock*, 173.

52. See Eileen McDonagh, "My Body, My Consent: Securing the Constitutional Right to Abortion Funding," *Albany Law Review* 62, 3 (1999):1085–88. Compare West, "Liberalism and Abortion," 2130.

53. See for example, Science and Technology Subgroup, "In the Wake of the Alton Bill: Science, Technology and Reproductive Politics," in, *Off-Centre: Feminism and Cultural Studies*, ed. Sarah Franklin, Celia Lury, and Jackie Stacey (London: HarperCollins Academic, 1991), 189.

54. McDonagh, *Breaking the Abortion Deadlock*, 70, 74–76, 145, and 169. Emphasis mine.

55. Ibid., 142. Emphasis mine.

56. Robin West, "Liberalism and Abortion," 2127.

57. McDonagh, *Breaking the Abortion Deadlock*, chapter 2.

58. Roger Wertheimer, "Understanding the Abortion Argument," in Feinberg, *The Problem of Abortion*, 54.

59. I have in mind particularly: L. W. Sumner, "A Third Way," in Feinberg, *The Problem of Abortion*, 72.

60. Annette E. Clark, "Abortion and the Pied Piper of Compromise," *New York University Law Review* 68 (May 1993) (Lexis-Nexis document, obtained February 16, 2002).

61. For a history of the relationship between eugenics and birth control movements in the United States, see Dorothy Roberts, *Killing the Black Body: Race, Reproduction and the Meaning of Liberty* (New York: Pantheon Books, 1997), 56–103.

62. For a helpful summary of the issues raised by the selective abortion of disabled fetuses, see Susan Wendell, *The Rejected Body: Feminist Philosophical Reflections on Disability* (New York: Routledge, 1996), 151–56. Also see Joan Hume, "Disability, Feminism and Eugenics: Who Has the Right to Decide Who Should or Should Not Inhabit the World?" [online], paper presented at the Women's Electoral Lobby National Conference, University of Technology, Sydney, January 26, 1996, available: http://www.wwda.org.au/eugen.htm [January 20, 2002]. Rayna Rapp discusses the social and cultural contexts in which women make decisions about aborting fetuses diagnosed with a disability in her chapter "The disabled Fetal Imaginary," in Rayna Rapp, *Testing Women, Testing the Fetus: The Social Impact of Amniocentesis in America* (New York: Routledge, 2000), 129–64.

63. Mark Tushnet writes that "Governor Ronald Reagan objected to a provision in the [California's] proposed reform bill that would have allowed

abortions in cases of fetal defects. Because the bill still allowed abortions to preserve the woman's life or physical or mental health, its chief sponsor believed that removing the provisions that Reagan objected to would not make much difference. With that provision removed, Reagan signed the reform bill in June 1967." Mark Tushnet, *Abortion*, Constitutional Issues Series (New York: Facts on File, 1996), 49–50. Whatever Reagan's reasons were for opposing eugenic abortions—political expediency or his "pro-life" views—I find the compromise here an acceptable one. Approving abortions simply because of a fetal disability, rather than the suffering the disability might impose on the woman or fetus, reinforces the stigma of being disabled. Removing the eugenic exception implies that the problem is not with the fetus but with meeting the demands of supporting its life. Sometimes we cannot meet these demands, or on balance not meeting them would involve less suffering, but there is no reason to assume in advance that such demands are not worth meeting.

64. Martin Benjamin has also argued for developing a regulatory compromise similar to Blackmun's initial scheme. He notes that "pro-choice" activists may be more willing than "pro-life" advocates to accept a political compromise on abortion because the "pro-choice" view is a pluralistic one, whereas the "pro-life" view is absolutist. I think Benjamin is right, though of course many "pro-choice" activists saw *Roe* as a compromise. In the next chapter, I take up the issue of how to translate a morally moderate and pluralistic position on abortion into a public campaign for abortion rights. Like Benjamin, I believe "that there is no single world view and way of life that can claim to be uniquely supported by abstract reason or the 'facts'; and . . . that rationally irreconcilable conflict rooted in opposing world views and ways of life is a feature of social existence that must be acknowledged by any adequate conception of ethics." The existence of irreconcilable world views should also be acknowledged in a democratic society, and respect for and compromise among different views should be reached through democratic public dialogue. See Martin Benjamin, *Splitting the Difference: Compromise and Integrity in Ethics and Politics* (Lawrence: University of Kansas Press, 1990), 169.

Chapter 3

1. Ian Shapiro, *Principled Criticism* (Berkeley: University of California Press, 1990), 276.

2. This chapter is an expanded version of my article "From Reproductive Rights to Reproductive Barbie: Post-Porn Modernism and Abortion," *Feminist Studies* 28 (spring 2002): 61–93.

3. See for example, Kathy Rudy, *Beyond Pro-life and Pro-choice: Moral Diversity in the Abortion Debate* (Boston: Beacon Press, 1996), 89; and Rickie Solinger, *Beggars and Choosers: How the Politics of Choice Shapes Adoption, Abortion, and Welfare in the United States* (New York: Hill and Wang, 2001), 5.

4. Solinger, *Beggars and Choosers*, 5.

5. Maud Lavin, *Clean New World: Culture, Politics, and Graphic Design* (Cambridge: MIT Press, 2001), 155.

6. These items and more are on sale at "Victory Won" [online], available: http://www.victory1.com/bumper_stickers.htm (January 19, 2002).

7. Figure 3.4 is from the organization Lancaster Life [online], available: http://www.lancasterlife.com/dead_babies.html (January 19, 2002). Figure 3.5 is from the "Genocide Awareness Project" (GAP) of The Center for Bio-Ethical Reform [online], available: http://www.cbrinfo.org/gap_signs.html (January 19, 2002).

8. Perhaps noting the rhetorical dilemmas posed by "choice" language, Carole Joffe entitles her review of Solinger's book "Choosing Choice." See *Women's Review of Books* 19 (November 2001): 18.

9. At a recent conference on reproductive choice, I asked a representative from Planned Parenthood about the meaning of the "Responsible Choices" slogan, and she replied that it means we should trust women to make responsible choices. For more information on this campaign, see Planned Parenthood Votes! Washington [online], available: http://www.ppvw.org/reschoices.htm (January 19, 2002).

10. The banner in figure 3.6 is from the Pro-Choice Public Education Project [online], available: http://www.protectchoice.org/index.html (January 19, 2002).

11. Kristin Luker, *Abortion and the Politics of Motherhood* (Berkeley: University of California, 1984), 241.

12. Lavin, *Clean New World*, 145.

13. The Center for the Study of Political Graphics is in Los Angeles; their web address is: http://www.politicalgraphics.org/ (January 19, 2002). Figure 3.10 is from the Pro-Choice Public Education Project [online], available: http://www.protectchoice.org/pepmedia2.html (January 19, 2002). Figure 3.11 is from a website maintained by mymblemy@yahoo.com and titled "Abortion: What Do You Think?" [online], available: http://www.geocities.com/Athens/Styx/9699/art.html (January 19, 2002).

14. I am grateful to Peter Ross for bringing the photograph in figure 3.12 to my attention. The "GAP" sign is from the Center for Bio-Ethical Reform [online], available: http://www.cbrinfo.org/gap.html (January 19, 2002).

15. "Abortion: What Do You Think?" [online], available: http://www.geocities.com/Athens/Styx/9699/art.html (January 19, 2002).

16. Some of the best known are: "The Unseen" by the Geto Boys (on *Uncut Dope*, Priority Records, 1992), "To Zion" by Lauryn Hill (on *The Miseducation of Lauryn Hill*, Ruff House/Columbia, 1998), "Retrospect for Life" by Common Sense (on *One Day It'll All Make Sense*, Relativity Records, 1997), "Abortion Is a Crime" by Alpha Blondy and the Solar System (on *Dieu*, World Pacific/Capital, 1994), "Abortion" by Yellowman (on *Freedom of Speech*, RAS Records, 1997), "Abortion" by Doug E. Fresh and the Get Fresh Crew (on *Louder Than a Bomb*, Rhino Entertainment, 1999). I am grateful to my former student, Jamaar Boyd, for alerting me to some of this music about abortion.

17. For a discussion of the "pro-life" video *The Silent Scream*, see Rosalind

Pollack Petchesky, "Fetal Images: The Power of Visual Culture in the Politics of Reproduction," *Feminist Studies* 13, 2 (summer 1987): 265–71. For discussions of fetal images in popular films, see Zoë Sofia, "Exterminating Fetuses: Abortion, Disarmament, and the Sexo-Semiotics of Extraterrestrialism," *Diacritics* 14 (summer 1984): 47–59; and Lauren Berlant, "America, Fat, the Fetus," *Boundary 2* 21, 3 (fall 1994): 145–95.

18. In a *San Jose Mercury News* story on April 25, 1999 (7A), entitled "Antiabortion Plea Targets Young Adults," Rose Ciotta describes an activist group called "Survivors," which was created by Operation Rescue activists in order to attract those born after *Roe v. Wade* to the "pro-life" movement.

19. For example, see Lancaster Life [online], available: http://www.lancasterlife.com/ (January 19, 2002).

20. Tom Lehrer, "The Folk Song Army" (on *That Was the Year That Was*, Reprise Records, 1965).

21. The music group Digable Planets refers to clinic protesters as "fascists" in their song "La Femme Fetal," one of the few recent popular pro-choice songs: " The pro-lifers harass me outside the clinic / and call me a murderer . . . / hey beautiful bird I said digging her somber mood / the fascists are some heavy dudes / they don't really give a damn about life / they just don't want a woman to / control her body or have the right to choose / . . . fire-bombing clinics / what type of shit is that? Orwellian in fact / if *Roe v. Wade* was overturned, would not the desire remain intact / leaving young girls to risk their health / and doctors to botch and watch as they kill themselves / now I don't want to sound macabre / but hey isn't it my job / to lay it on the masses and get them off their asses / to fight against these fascists"; on *Reachin' (A New Refutation of Time and Space)*, Capitol Records, 1993. These lyrics are from The Original Hip-Hop Lyrics Archive (http://ohhla.com/) at: http://ohhla.com/anonymous/digablep/reachin/femme.pln.txt The reproductive rights movement has generated some good songs about clinic violence and the murder of abortion providers, as well as moving, thoughtful ballads about women who have died from illegal abortions. For example, see Ani DiFranco, "Hello Birmingham" (on *To the Teeth*, Righteous Babe Records, 1999), which addresses clinic violence. For songs about women who died from illegal abortions, see Cyndi Lauper, "Sally's Pigeon's" (on *Hat Full of Stars*, Epic Records, 1993) and Peggy Seeger, "Judge's Chair (on *An Odd Collection*, Rounder Records, 1996). Also see DiFranco's earlier "Lost Woman Song" (on *Like I Said*, Righteous Babe Records, 1993), which offers a woman's complex thoughts as she seeks an abortion. As to which group has the most moving or musically interesting songs, these artists or those mentioned in note 16, I will leave this question to the music critics.

22. Lavin, *Clean New World*, 155.

23. Rosalind Pollack Petchesky, *Abortion and a Woman's Choice: The State, Sexuality, and Reproductive Freedom*, rev. ed. (Boston: Northeastern University Press, 1990 [1984]). Also see Petchesky, "Fetal Images," 264.

24. Petchesky, *Abortion and a Woman's Choice*, especially xi, and 338–42.

25. Ibid., xiv, and Petchesky, "Fetal Images," 264.
26. Petchesky, *Abortion and a Woman's Choice*, x.
27. Petchesky "Fetal Images," 287.
28. Lucy Lippard, *The Pink Glass Swan: Selected Essays on Feminist Art* (New York: New Press, 1995), 250.
29. Petchesky, "Fetal Images," 264.
30. The Science and Technology Subgroup, "In the Wake of the Alton Bill: Science, Technology and Reproductive Politics," in *Off-Centre: Feminism and Cultural Studies*, ed. Sarah Franklin, Celia Lury, and Jackie Stacy (London: HarperCollins Academic, 1991), 147.
31. Ibid., 215.
32. Sarah Franklin, "Fetal Fascinations: New Dimensions to the Medical-Scientific Construction of Fetal Personhood," in Franklin, Lury, and Stacy, *Off-Centre*, 191.
33. Ibid., 191 and 200.
34. Ibid., 203.
35. Deborah Lynn Steinberg, "Adversarial Politics: The Legal Construction of Abortion," in Franklin, Lury, and Stacy, *Off-Centre*, 189.
36. Valerie Hartouni, *Cultural Conceptions: On Reproductive Technologies and the Remaking of Life* (Minneapolis: University of Minnesota Press, 1997).
37. Ibid., 34–35. Petchesky, "Fetal Images," 264, notes the prevalence of fetal images that "float like spirits" in courtrooms, hospitals, bus terminals, and so on.
38. Petchesky, "Fetal Images," 268, and 271–86. See also Barbara Duden, "Joanne and Susan," in *Disembodying Women: Perspectives on Pregnancy and the Unborn* (Cambridge: Harvard University Press, 1993), 30–33; and Monica Caspar, *The Making of the Unborn Patient* (New Brunswick, NJ: Rutgers University Press, 1998).
39. Hartouni, *Cultural Conceptions*, 24.
40. See Eileen McDonagh, *Breaking the Abortion Deadlock: From Choice to Consent* (New York: Oxford University Press, 1996), throughout.
41. Hartouni, *Cultural Conceptions*, 67.
42. Karen Newman, *Fetal Positions: Individualism, Science, Visuality* (Stanford: Stanford University Press, 1996), 26.
43. Ibid., 27. See also Barbara Stafford, *Imaging the Unseen in Enlightenment Art and Medicine* (Cambridge: MIT Press, 1993), 240–48.
44. Barbara Duden, "The Fetus on the 'Farther Shore,'" in *Fetal Subjects, Feminist Positions*, ed. Lynn Morgan and Meredith Michaels (Philadelphia: University of Pennsylvania Press, 1999), 21.
45. Newman, *Fetal Positions*, 110.
46. See also Janelle Taylor, "The Public Fetus and the Family Car: From Abortion Politics to a Volvo Advertisement," in *Public Culture* 4, 2 (spring 1992): 75–76.
47. Newman, *Fetal Positions*, 110–13.
48. Meredith Michaels writes: "In the context of contentions over abortion, the question is: who is more real, women or fetuses? The feminist repro-

ductive rights movement could be viewed as an effort to elevate women's ontological ranking by recasting them as agents capable of choice." See her "Fetal Galaxies: Some Questions about What We See," in Morgan and Michaels, *Fetal Subjects, Feminist Positions*, 117.

49. I am grateful to Karen Barad for calling my attention to 3D ultrasound and its possible impact on the abortion debate. Figure 3.16 is from "Take a Look at the Future of Ultrasound" [online], available: http://www. fetus.com/3DUS2.html (January 19, 2002). Also see Karen Barad, "Getting Real: Technoscientific Practices and the Materialization of Reality," *Differences* 10, 2 (summer 1998): 87–128.

50. Lynn Morgan, "Fetal Relationality in Feminist Philosophy: An Anthropological Critique," *Hypatia* 11, 3 (summer 1996): 63.

51. I'm drawing inspiration here from Judith Butler's work on denaturalizing gender categories.

52. Lisa M. Mitchell and Eugenia Georges, "Cross-cultural Cyborgs: Greek and Canadian Women's Discourses on Fetal Ultrasound," *Feminist Studies* 23, 2 (summer 1997): 397.

53. James Brooke, "Canada Sees Abortion War Turn Violent, Services Fall," *New York Times*, July 16, 2000.

54. Jana Sawicki, *Disciplining Foucault: Feminism, Power and the Body* (New York: Routledge, 1991), 89.

55. Janelle S. Taylor, "Image of Contradiction: Obstetrical Ultrasound in American Culture," in *Reproducing Reproduction: Kinship, Power, and Technological Innovation*, ed. Sarah Franklin and Helena Ragoné (Philadelphia: University of Pennsylvania Press, 1998), 15–45.

56. Ibid., 21.

57. In discussing the role of amniocentesis in raising "production standards," Barbara Katz Rothman considers the pressure women face to get tested or to selectively abort disabled fetuses. Barbara Katz Rothman, *The Tentative Pregnancy: How Amniocentesis Changes the Experience of Motherhood* (New York: Norton, 1993), 227. See also Rayna Rapp, "The Disabled Fetal Imaginary," in *Testing Women, Testing the Fetus: The Social Impact of Amniocentesis in America* (New York: Routledge, 2000), 129–64.

58. Bruno Latour, "Visualization and Cognition," in *Knowledge and Society: Studies in the Sociology of Culture Past and Present*, vol. 6, ed. Henrika Kuklick and Elizabeth Long (Greenwich, CT: JAI Press, 1986), 1–40. See also Newman, *Fetal Positions*, 7–8.

59. Latour, "Visualization and Cognition," 14.

60. Michaels, "Fetal Galaxies," 119.

61. Duden, *Disembodying Women*, 25.

62. Ibid., 17.

63. Faye Ginsburg, *Contested Lives: The Abortion Debate in an American Community* (Berkeley: University of California Press, 1989), 104.

64. Latour, "Visualization and Cognition," 17. According to Celeste Condit, "in the early period of the controversy advocates brought pickled fetuses in jars to legislative hearings. In the middle period packets of photographs presented the image. In the later period the photographs were more

widely disseminated in mass media and on billboards" *Decoding Abortion Rhetoric: Communicating Social Change* (Urbana: University of Illinois Press, 1990), 82.

65. In the course of writing this chapter, this controversial site has moved around the internet. I recently found the Nuremberg Files at: http://www.christiangallery.com/atrocity/ (January 19, 2002).

66. Latour, "Visualization and Cognition," 18.

67. *Leona's Sister Gerri*, A Documentary Film by Jane Gillooly, New Day Films, 1994.

68. Celeste Condit writes: "Skillful selection and contextualization were vital influences on the creation of this rhetorical image of 'the fetus,' but the most important influence was simply that of verbal commentary. Without verbal commentary, the "pictures DO NOT ARGUE propositions. An image may suggest 'this looks like x," but the assertion of identity, that 'this IS x,' must be verbally supplied. In terms of argument theory, a picture provides the substance for a ground, but the precise ground must be made verbally explicit and a claim must be supplied for the rhetor to control the process of inference." *Decoding Abortion Rhetoric*, 85. Although verbal commentary conjoined to an image or provided by the purveyor of an image plays an important role in directing the initial reception of the image, I wonder, especially once the image and its associated message has become familiar, whether the image alone can possess argumentative force. In other words, I'm inclined to agree with Latour and Duden that images may play a direct role in rationally persuading us of particular views, and they perhaps serve to mediate our reception of verbal propositions as much as the latter mediate our reception of images. If something can be visualized, we are more likely to believe it, suggesting that the image does as much work as the accompanying text.

69. Center for the Study of Political Graphics, Los Angeles.

70. See Carol Stabile, *Feminism and the Technological Fix* (Manchester, England: Manchester University Press, 1994), 94.

71. Linda Layne, "Breaking the Silence: An Agenda for a Feminist Discourse of Pregnancy Loss," *Feminist Studies* 23, 2 (summer 1997): 305.

72. According to Andrzej Kulczycki, in developing countries "the risk of death from childbirth is at least 11 times higher, and 30 times higher than for abortions up to eight weeks of gestation." See his *The Abortion Debate in the World Arena* (New York: Routledge, 1999), 5.

73. See Barbara Kruger, *Thinking of You* (Cambridge: MIT Press, 1999), 24, 70–71, and 223. Lucy Lippard discusses these posters in *The Pink Glass Swan*, 251. Imagine new versions of figure 3.23, e.g., George W. Bush: "The war on terrorism is going great, my approval ratings are soaring, and I need to get Saddam, but I just found out I'm pregnant. . . ." Or John Ashcroft: " I'm moving the conservative Christian Agenda forward, I've got hundreds of detainees to get rid of while liberals are screaming about civil rights, but I just found out I'm pregnant . . ."

74. Their posters can be viewed online at: http://www.guerrillagirls.com/posters/poster_index.html (January 19, 2002). Another Guerrilla Girls

poster says "Guerrilla Girls Demand a Return to Traditional Values on Abortion: Before the mid-19th century, abortion in the first few months of pregnancy was legal. Even the Catholic Church did not forbid it until 1869." This poster usefully points out that the Catholic Church has not always been opposed to all abortions. However, one might argue back that laws and moralities often change and sometimes for the better, such as with slavery.

75. Jean Reith Schroedel, *Is the Fetus a Person? A Comparison of Policies across the Fifty States* (Ithaca, NY: Cornell University Press, 2000).

76. Parts of Lisa Link's Warnings exhibit are online at: http://babel.massart. edu/~llink/html/exhibitFrame.html (January 19, 2002).

77. "ADL Investigation Reveals Strain of Anti-Semitism in Extreme Factions of the Anti-Abortion Movement," [online], October 30, 1998, available: http://www.adl.org/presrele/asus_12/3265_12.asp (February 15, 2002).

78. Lippard, *The Pink Glass Swan*, 250.

79. Kruger, *Thinking of You*, 62–63, 69, 117, and 242.

80. Barbara Kruger gave the PCPEP and their ad agency, DeVito/Verdi, permission to create posters in the style of her work. Later, she included some of their posters in exhibits of her work at the Musuem of Contemporary Art in Los Angeles, and at the Whitney Museum in New York, in order to illustrate how her ideas have been taken up by others. When an attribution to the ad agency was by mistake left off the wall at the Whitney, the ad agency threatened to sue Kruger instead of simply asking the museum to include the credit line (and which Kruger says would have been done immediately if the omission had been brought to their attention). Ironically, the DeVito/Verdi ads, which copy her style and work, do not include a credit line with Kruger's name. Kruger has in the past offered to create artwork for groups like NARAL and Planned Parenthood, and they have turned her down. However, when she produced "Your body is a battleground" on her own, organizations such as the PCPEP and their constituent groups used and appropriated it, which Kruger is happy to have them do. From a phone call with Kruger, 4/19/02. For the PCPEP posters, see "lastpage," *Ms.* 9, 3 (April/May 1999). I am grateful to Diana Linden for alerting me to this issue of *Ms.* These images can also be viewed at the Pro-Choice Public Education Project [online], available: http://www.protectchoice.org/pepmedia2.html (January 19, 2002).

81. Lisa Link, "Warnings" [online], available: http://babel.massart. edu/~llink/html/exhibitFrame.html, click on "Gallery Views" (January 19, 2002); also see the L.A. guerilla artist Robbie Conal's poster satirizing the "gag rule," "Gag me with a Coat Hanger" [online], available: http://secure.labridge.com/msbooks/conal.gagme.html (January 19, 2002). I am grateful to Gail Sansbury for alerting me to this poster.

82. *Feminist Studies* 23, 2 (summer 1997), 316. High's "Trangenic Fantascope" is on the cover of the same issue.

83. Sarah Franklin, "Dead Embryos: Feminism in Suspension," in Morgan and Michaels, *Fetal Subjects, Feminist Positions*, 73.

84. *Animals' Agenda* 18 (May/June 1998): 22–29. See also Carol J. Adams,

"Abortion Rights and Animal Rights," in *Neither Man nor Beast: Feminism and the Defense of Animals* (New York: Continuum, 1994), 55–70.

85. Liz McQuiston, *Suffragettes to She-Devils: Women's Liberation and Beyond* (London: Phaidon Press, 1997), 143 and 147.

86. Sue Coe, *Dead Meat* (New York: Four Walls Eight Windows, 1995).

87. Ibid., fourth image occurring between pages 40 and 41. Another Coe image features bubbles containing animals positioned around a meat grinder. Sue Coe, "Untitled," 1997, National Museum of Women in the Arts [online], available: http://www.nmwa.org/shop/prints/pcoe.htm (January 19, 2002).

88. Although "pro-life" activists have used these analogies for some time (e.g., see Condit, *Decoding Abortion Rhetoric*, 49), I'm not sure when the images I'm describing first began to appear or how widely they're used.

89. See the "American-Nazi War Memorial" [online], available: http://www.mttu.com/memorial/index.html (January 19, 2002). Also see the "American Holocaust Memorial" [online], available: http://www. thekingsnetwork.com/holocaust/ (January 19, 2002). In addition, see "The American Holocaust" [online], available: http://www.familybible. org/Articles/WorldEvents/Abortion.htm (January 19, 2002); and "Nazi Connection" at "Abortion is Murder" [online], available: http://abortionismurder.org/index.shtml (January 19, 2002).

90. GAP Signs, Center for Bio-Ethical Reform [online], available: http://www.cbrinfo.org/gap_signs.html (January 19, 2002).

91. Liz McQuiston, *Suffragettes to She-Devils*, 154. I am grateful to Jessica Lawless and Mary Ellen Croteau, both artists who were involved with Sister Serpents, for informing me about the context that led to this poster. Croteau says the fetus photo was taken by a member of Sister Serpents at the Chicago Museum of Science and Industry from a jar displaying a fetus. The poster was mailed to activists and publications around the world, as well as wheat-pasted around Chicago. From private correspondence with Croteau, May 2002.

92. I am grateful to Jessica Lawless for lending me her copies of *Madwoman*. These images are from issue #3, Spring 1992. Helena Perkins, the publisher of the zine *Madwoman*, which published eleven issues from 1991–98, recalls that the "Baby Vanishes" image was sent to her by someone who clipped it from the *National Inquirer*. So it may not be a parody but the real thing. Perkins says that Sister Serpents was active until the mid-1990s and that the group was the inspiration of the artist Jeremy Turner who wanted to address misogyny through art. Turner organized art exhibits, and some Sister Serpent artists got involved with radio and stage shows, and a billboard ad. Other artists developed posters and stickers, which were put up around the city, and Perkins started the zine *Madwoman* in this context. From private correspondence with Perkins, May 2002.

93. Dorothy Jiji, "The Story of the Hanger," in "Reproductive Choice: Obstacles to Self-Determination," curated by Sachiko Onishi, exhibit held at the Art Resources Transfer, New York City, June 25–August 27, 1999. I

am grateful to Dorothy Jiji, who sent me photos of her work, although the photo in figure 3.37 was taken by my mother, who visited this exhibit.

94. I am grateful to Nancy Kolman for this suggestion.

95. Shannon Bell, *Reading, Writing, and Rewriting the Prostitute Body* (Bloomington: Indiana University Press, 1994), 176.

96. Ibid., 177.

97. Ibid., 177. For more information on Carol Leigh's films, see "The Collected Work of Scarlot Harlot" [online], available: http://www.bayswan.org/Scarlot_Videos.html (January 19, 2002).

98. Peggy Phelan, "White Men and Pregnancy: Discovering the Body to Be Rescued," in *Acting Out: Feminist Performances,* ed. Lynda Hart and Peggy Phelan (Ann Arbor: University of Michigan Press, 1993), 383–84.

99. "Welcome to My World," *Women's Review of Books* 19 (December 2001): 8.

100. Brett Harvey, "No More Nice Girls," in *Pleasure and Danger: Exploring Female Sexuality,* ed. Carol Vance (London: Pandora Press, 1989), 206.

101. Rather than stage pregnancy as a form of slavery, performance protests might try parodying "pro-life" protests in order to call attention to what antiabortion groups are doing with their performances. Imagine a group of protesters staging a "rescue" at a store that sells Beanie Babies, with signs that say "Pro-Toy," "It's a toy, not an investment," and "Choose Play." A more serious "rescue" operation might involve a protest at a public welfare agency to call attention to the tragic consequences of inadequate levels of assistance to single mothers and their children. A simple street demostration could involve pregnant men standing behind "HELP" signs in the style of Barbara Kruger.

102. Bell, *Reading, Writing, and Rewriting the Prostitute Body,* 152. See also Annie Sprinkle, *Post-porn Modernist: My First Twenty-five Years as a Multi-media Whore* (San Francisco: Cleis Press, 1998).

103. Bell's description of Sprinkle's performance aptly characterizes other first-person accounts I've heard. Unfortunately, I have never attended one of these performances.

104. However, Sprinkle now has a website where viewers can see a "cervix shot": http://gatesofheck.com/annie/gallery/cervixmain.html [January 19, 2002].

105. Sarah Strohmeyer, *Barbie Unbound: A Parody of Barbie Obsession* (Norwich, VT: New Victoria, 1997).

106. From "Barbies We'd Like to See" [online], available: http://www.personal.psu.edu/staff/k/e/kej113/barbies.html (January 19, 2002). Many of the sites I have visited since 1998 no longer exist, although if you type "Barbie" into a search engine, such as Google.com, you will find new ones. The video *Barbie Nation: An Unauthorized Tour,* by Susan Stern (New Day Films, 1998), also features some alternative Barbies.

107. Duden, *Disembodying Women,* 17.

108. I created the images in figures 3.39–3.46 with a scanner and simple com-

puter graphics software. I am not a graphic artist, and these images are intended to encourage others with more talent to produce new reproductive rights imagery.

109. Lynda Hart, introduction to Hart and Phelan, *Acting Out*, 11.

110. Iris Schilke has informed me about an action started in Dresden, Germany, called "Mail-Art gegen §218" (in 1993) that involved men and women creating "pro-choice" postcards. She has very kindly mailed me a packet of these postcards, with an accompanying description (in German) of the project. This action suggests one relatively easy way to get feminist images into wider circulation.

Chapter 4

1. Ruth Bader Ginsburg, "Speaking in a Judicial Voice," *New York University Law Review* 67 (December 1992) (Lexis-Nexis document, obtained February 16, 2002).

2. Ibid.

3. Ibid.

4. Ibid.

5. Alissa J. Rubin, "Americans Narrowing Support for Abortions," *Los Angeles Times* [online], June 18, 2000, available: http://www.latimes.com/news/custom/timespoll/la-000618abortpoll.story (January 21, 2002).

6. Annette E. Clark, "Abortion and the Pied Piper of Compromise," *New York University Law Review* 68 (May 1993) (Lexis-Nexis document, obtained February 16, 2002).

7. Clyde Wilcox and Julia Riches, "Pills in the Public's Mind: RU 486 and the Framing of the Abortion Issue," unpublished article.

8. Ibid., and also see Rubin, "Americans Narrowing Support for Abortions."

9. See, for example, Lawrence H. Tribe, *Abortion: The Clash of Absolutes* (New York: Norton, 1992), 75. Also see Kristin Luker, *Abortion and the Politics of Motherhood* (Berkeley: University of California, 1984), 45–46, and 76–91.

10. The bottom of the flier identifies the organization that produced it: "Heritage House '76, Pro-Family Pro-Life Research Center, P.O. Box 730, Taylor, AZ 85939." I found the following "pro-life" website with this name: http://www.heritagehouse76.com/.

11. These lyrics are from The Original Hip-Hop Lyrics Archive (http://ohhla.com/) at: http://www.ohhla.com/anonymous/lauryn/tmolh/to_zion.fge.txt.

Bibliography

Abortion Law Reform Association (ALRA). "The Campaign for Choice."
    Online. Available: http://www.alra.org.uk/whychan.html. January 19,
    2002.
Adams, Carol J. "Abortion Rights and Animal Rights." In *Neither Man nor
    Beast: Feminism and the Defense of Animals*, 55–70. New York: Con-
    tinuum, 1994.
Allen, Anita. "Privacy and Equal Protection as Bases for Abortion Law." In
    *Having and Raising Children: Unconventional Families, Hard Choices,
    and the Social Good*, ed. Uma Narayan and Julia J. Bartkowiak, 119–136.
    University Park: Pennsylvania State University Press, 1999.
Barad, Karen. "Getting Real: Technoscientific Practices and the Materialization
    of Reality." *Differences* 10, 2 (summer 1998): 87–128.
Bell, Shannon. *Reading, Writing, and Rewriting the Prostitute Body*. Bloom-
    ington: Indiana University Press, 1994.
Benjamin, Martin. *Splitting the Difference: Compromise and Integrity in
    Ethics and Politics*. Lawrence: University of Kansas Press, 1990.
Berlant, Lauren. "America, Fat, the Fetus." *Boundary 2* 21, 3 (fall 1994):
    145–95.
Bickel, Alexander. *The Morality of Consent*. New Haven: Yale University
    Press, 1975.
Blake, Judith. "The Abortion Decisions: Judicial Review and Public Opinion."
    In *Abortion: New Directions for Policy Studies*, ed. Edward Manier,
    William Lu, and David Solomon, 51–82. Notre Dame, IN: University of
    Notre Dame Press, 1977.
Blank, Robert. "Judicial Decision Making and Biological Fact: *Roe v. Wade* and
    the Unresolved Question of Fetal Viability." *Western Political Quarterly*
    37 (1984): 584–602.
Boss, Judith. *Analyzing Moral Issues* 2nd ed. Boston: McGraw-Hill, 2002.
Brodie, Janet Farrell. *Conception and Abortion in Nineteenth-Century
    America*. Ithaca: Cornell University Press, 1994.
Caspar, Monica. *The Making of the Unborn Patient*. New Brunswick, NJ: Rut-
    gers University Press, 1998.
Center for Reproductive Law and Policy. *The World's Abortion Laws 2000*.
    New York: CRLP, 2000.
Clark, Annette E. "Abortion and the Pied Piper of Compromise." *New York*

University Law Review 68 (May 1993). (Lexis-Nexis document, obtained February 16, 2002.)

Clark, Carole. "Perspectives of Viability," *Arizona State Law Journal* 12 (1980): 128–59.

Coe, Sue. *Dead Meat.* New York: Four Walls Eight Windows, 1995.

Colker, Ruth. *Abortion and Dialogue.* Bloomington: Indiana University Press, 1992.

Condit, Celeste. *Decoding Abortion Rhetoric: Communicating Social Change.* Urbana: University of Illinois Press, 1990.

Davis, Michael D., and Hunter R. Clark. *Thurgood Marshall: Warrior at the Bar, Rebel on the Bench.* New York: Birch Lane Press, 1992.

Davis, Nancy. "Abortion and Self Defense." In *Abortion: Moral and Legal Perspectives,* ed. Jay Garfield and Patricia Hennessey, 186–210. Amherst: University of Massachusetts Press, 1984.

Deflem, Mathieu. "The Boundaries of Abortion Law: Systems Theories from Parsons to Luhmann and Habermas." *Social Forces* 76 (1998): 775–818.

Dellinger, Walter, and Gene Sperling. "Abortion and the Supreme Court: The Retreat from *Roe v. Wade.*" *University of Pennsylvania Law Review* 138 (November 1989): 83–118.

Duden, Barbara. *Disembodying Women: Perspectives on Pregnancy and the Unborn.* Cambridge: Harvard University Press, 1993.

———. "The Fetus on the 'Farther Shore.'" In *Fetal Subjects, Feminist Positions,* ed. Lynn Morgan and Meredith Michaels, 13–25. Philadelphia: University of Pennsylvania Press, 1999.

Dworkin, Ronald. *Life's Dominion: An Argument about Abortion, Euthanasia, and Individual Freedom.* New York: Knopf, 1993.

Franklin, Sarah. "Fetal Fascinations: New Dimensions to the Medical-Scientific Construction of Fetal Personhood." In *Off-Centre: Feminism and Cultural Studies,* ed. Sarah Franklin, Celia Lury, and Jackie Stacy, 190–205. London: HarperCollins Academic, 1991.

———. "Dead Embryos: Feminism in Suspension." In *Fetal Subjects, Feminist Positions,* ed. Lynn Morgan and Meredith Michaels, 61–82. Philadelphia: University of Pennsylvania Press, 1999.

Fried, Marlene Gerber. "Abortion in the United States: Legal but Inaccessible." In *Abortion Wars: A Half Century of Struggle, 1950–2000,* ed. Rickie Solinger, 208–226. Berkeley: University of California Press, 1998.

Garrow, David. *Liberty and Sexuality.* New York: Macmillan, 1994.

———. "Revelations on the Road to *Roe.*" *American Lawyer* (May 2000): 80–83.

Garry, Ann. "Abortion: Models of Responsibility," *Law and Philosophy* 2 (1983): 371–96.

Gert, Heather. "Viability." In *The Problem of Abortion,* ed. Joel Feinberg, 3rd ed., 118–126. Belmont, CA: Wadsworth, 1997.

Ginsburg, Faye. *Contested Lives: The Abortion Debate in an American Community.* Berkeley: University of California Press, 1989.

Ginsburg, Ruth Bader, "Speaking in a Judicial Voice," New York University

Law Review 67 (December 1992). (Lexis-Nexis document, obtained February 16, 2002.)

Glendon, Mary Ann. *Abortion and Divorce in Western Law*. Cambridge: Harvard University Press, 1987.

Hartouni, Valerie. *Cultural Conceptions: On Reproductive Technologies and the Remaking of Life*. Minneapolis: University of Minnesota Press, 1997.

Harvey, Brett. "No More Nice Girls." In *Pleasure and Danger: Exploring Female Sexuality*, ed. Carol Vance, 204–9. London: Pandora Press, 1989.

Hoff, Joan. *Law, Gender, and Injustice: A Legal History of U.S. Women*. New York: New York University Press, 1991.

Houppert, Karen. "For Her Own Good," *The Nation* (February 4, 2002): 20–24.

Hull, N. E. H., and Peter Charles Hoffer. *Roe v. Wade: The Abortion Rights Controversy in American History*. Lawrence: University of Kansas Press, 2001.

Hume, Joan. "Disability, Feminism and Eugenics: Who Has the Right to Decide Who Should or Should Not Inhabit the World?" Paper presented at the Women's Electoral Lobby National Conference, University of Technology, Sydney, January 26, 1996. Online. Available: http://www.wwda.org.au/eugen.htm. January 20, 2002.

Jaggar, Alison. "Abortion and a Woman's Right to Decide." In *Women and Philosophy: Toward a Theory of Liberation*, ed. Carol Gould and Marx Wartofsky, 347–60. New York: Capricorn Books, 1976.

Joffe, Carole. "Choosing Choice." *Women's Review of Books* 19 (November 2001): 18–19.

Kamm, F. M. *Creation and Abortion: A Study in Moral and Legal Philosophy*. New York: Oxford University Press, 1992.

Kommers, Donald P. "Abortion and the Constitution: The Cases of the United States and West Germany." In *Abortion: New Directions for Policy Studies*, ed. Edward Manier, William Lu, and David Solomon, 83–116. Notre Dame, IN: University of Notre Dame Press, 1977.

———. *The Constitutional Jurisprudence of the Federal Republic of Germany* 2nd ed. Durham, NC: Duke University Press, 1997.

Kruger, Barbara. *Thinking of You*. Cambridge: MIT Press, 1999.

Kulczycki, Andrzej. *The Abortion Debate in the World Arena*. New York: Routledge, 1999.

Ladd, Everett Carll, and Karlyn H. Bowman. *Public Opinion about Abortion: Twenty-five Years after Roe v. Wade*. Washington, DC: American Enterprise Institute Press, 1997.

Latour, Bruno. "Visualization and Cognition." In *Knowledge and Society: Studies in the Sociology of Culture Past and Present*, vol. 6, ed. Henrika Kuklick and Elizabeth Long, 1–40. Greenwich, CT: JAI Press, 1986.

Lavin, Maud. *Clean New World: Culture, Politics, and Graphic Design*. Cambridge: MIT Press, 2001.

Law, Sylvia. "Abortion Compromise—Inevitable but Impossible." *University of Illinois Law Review* (1992). (Lexis-Nexis document, obtained September 1, 2001.)

Layne, Linda. "Breaking the Silence: An Agenda for a Feminist Discourse of Pregnancy Loss." *Feminist Studies* 23, 2 (summer 1997): 289–315.

Lippard, Lucy. *The Pink Glass Swan: Selected Essays on Feminist Art.* New York: New Press, 1995.

Little, Margaret Olivia. "Abortion, Intimacy, and the Duty to Gestate," *Ethical Theory and Moral Practice* 2 (1999): 295–312.

Luker, Kristin. *Abortion and the Politics of Motherhood.* Berkeley: University of California Press, 1984.

McClain, Linda C. "'Atomistic Man' Revisited: Liberalism, Connection, and Feminist Jurisprudence." *Southern California Law Review* 65 (March 1992). (Lexis-Nexis document, obtained March 2002.)

McDonagh, Eileen. *Breaking the Abortion Deadlock: From Choice to Consent.* New York: Oxford University Press, 1996.

———. "My Body, My Consent: Securing the Constitutional Right to Abortion Funding." *Albany Law Review* 62, 3 (1999): 1085–88.

McMahan, Jeff. "The Right to Choose an Abortion." *Philosophy and Public Affairs* 22, (fall 1993): 331–48.

McQuiston, Liz. *Suffragettes to She-Devils: Women's Liberation and Beyond.* London: Phaidon Press, 1997.

Michaels, Meredith. "Abortion and the Claims of Samaritanism." In *Abortion: Moral and Legal Perspectives,* ed. Jay Garfield and Patricia Hennessey, 213–26. Amherst: University of Massachusetts Press, 1984.

———. "Fetal Galaxies: Some Questions about What We See." In *Fetal Subjects, Feminist Positions,* ed. Lynn Morgan and Meredith Michaels, 113–32. Philadelphia: University of Pennsylvania Press, 1999.

Mitchell, Lisa M., and Eugenia Georges. "Cross-cultural Cyborgs: Greek and Canadian Women's Discourses on Fetal Ultrasound." *Feminist Studies* 23, 2 (summer 1997): 373–401.

Morgan, Lynn. "Fetal Relationality in Feminist Philosophy: An Anthropological Critique." *Hypatia* 11, 3 (summer 1996): 47–70.

Newman, Karen. *Fetal Positions: Individualism, Science, Visuality.* Stanford: Stanford University Press, 1996.

Ortiz, Ana Teresa. "'Bare-Handed' Medicine and Its Elusive Patients: The Unstable Construction of Pregnant Women and Fetuses in Dominican Obstetrics Discourse." *Feminist Studies* 23, 2 (summer 1997): 263–88.

Paul, Ellen Frankel, and Jeffrey Paul. "Self-ownership, Abortion and Infanticide." *Journal of Medical Ethics* 5 (1979): 133–38.

Petchesky, Rosalind Pollack. "Fetal Images: The Power of Visual Culture in the Politics of Reproduction." *Feminist Studies* 13, 2 (summer 1987): 263–92.

———. *Abortion and a Woman's Choice: The State, Sexuality, and Reproductive Freedom.* Rev. ed. Boston: Northeastern University Press, 1990 [1984].

Phelan, Peggy. "White Men and Pregnancy: Discovering the Body to Be Rescued." In *Acting Out: Feminist Performances,* ed. Lynda Hart and Peggy Phelan, 383–401. Ann Arbor: University of Michigan Press, 1993.

Planned Parenthood Affiliates of California. "Abortion and Fetal Viability."

May 1, 1997. Online. Available: http://www.ppacca.org/issues/
read.asp?ID=44. January 19, 2002.

Press, Andrea, and Elizabeth Cole. *Speaking of Abortion: Television and Authority in the Lives of Women*. Chicago: University of Chicago Press, 1999.

Rapp, Rayna. *Testing Women, Testing the Fetus: The Social Impact of Amniocentesis in America*. New York: Routledge, 2000.

Regan, Donald H. "Rewriting *Roe v. Wade*." *Michigan Law Review* 77 (August 1979): 1569–1646.

Reiman, Jeffrey. *Abortion and the Ways We Value Human Life*. Lanham, MD: Rowman and Littlefield, 1999.

Rhoden, Nancy K. "The New Neonatal Dilemma: Live Births from Late Abortions." *Georgetown Law Journal* 72 (June 1984). (Lexis-Nexis document, obtained July, 2001.)

————. "Trimesters and Technology: Revamping *Roe v. Wade*." *Yale Law Journal* 95 (March 1986): 639–97.

Roberts, Dorothy. *Killing the Black Body: Race, Reproduction and the Meaning of Liberty*. New York: Pantheon Books, 1997.

Rothman, Barbara Katz. *The Tentative Pregnancy: How Amniocentesis Changes the Experience of Motherhood*. New York: Norton, 1993.

Rubin, Alissa J. "Americans Narrowing Support for Abortions." *Los Angeles Times*, June 18, 2000. Online. Available: http://www.latimes.com/news/custom/timespoll/la-000618abortpoll.story. January 21, 2002.

Rubin, Eva R., ed. *The Abortion Controversy*. Westport, CT: Praeger, 1998.

Rudy, Kathy. *Beyond Pro-life and Pro-choice: Moral Diversity in the Abortion Debate*. Boston: Beacon Press, 1996.

Sawicki, Jana. *Disciplining Foucault: Feminism, Power and the Body*. New York: Routledge, 1991.

Schroedel, Jean Reith. *Is the Fetus a Person? A Comparison of Policies across the Fifty States*. Ithaca, NY: Cornell University Press, 2000.

Science and Technology Subgroup. "In the Wake of the Alton Bill: Science, Technology and Reproductive Politics." In *Off-Centre: Feminism and Cultural Studies*, ed. Sarah Franklin, Celia Lury, and Jackie Stacey, 149–218. London: HarperCollins Academic, 1991.

Shapiro, Ian. *Principled Criticism*. Berkeley: University of California Press, 1990.

Shrage, Laurie. "From Reproductive Rights to Reproductive Barbie: Post-*porn* Modernism and Abortion." *Feminist Studies* 28, 1 (spring 2002): 61–93.

Sofia, Zoë. "Exterminating Fetuses: Abortion, Disarmament, and the Sexo-Semiotics of Extraterrestrialism." *Diacritics* 14 (summer 1984): 47–59.

Solinger, Rickie, ed. *Abortion Wars: A Half Century of Struggle, 1950–2000*. Berkeley: University of California Press, 1998.

————. *Beggars and Choosers: How the Politics of Choice Shapes Adoption, Abortion, and Welfare in the United States*. New York: Hill and Wang, 2001.

Sprinkle, Annie. *Post-porn Modernist: My First Twenty-five Years as a Multimedia Whore*. San Francisco: Cleis Press, 1998.

Stabile, Carol. *Feminism and the Technological Fix*. Manchester, England: Manchester University Press, 1994.

Stafford, Barbara. *Imaging the Unseen in Enlightenment Art and Medicine*. Cambridge: MIT Press, 1993.

Steinberg, Deborah Lynn. "Adversarial Politics: the Legal Construction of Abortion." In *Off-Centre: Feminism and Cultural Studies*, ed. Sarah Franklin, Celia Lury, and Jackie Stacy, 175–89. London: HarperCollins Academic, 1991.

Strohmeyer, Sarah. *Barbie Unbound: A Parody of Barbie Obsession*. Norwich, VT: New Victoria, 1997.

Sumner, L. W. "A Third Way." In *The Problem of Abortion*, ed. Joel Feinberg, 2nd ed., 71–93. Belmont, CA: Wadsworth, 1984.

Sunstein, Cass. "Neutrality in Constitutional Law (with Special Reference to Pornography, Abortion, and Surrogacy)." *Columbia Law Review* 92 (January 1992): 1–52.

———. *Legal Reasoning and Political Conflict*. New York: Oxford University Press, 1996.

Taylor, Janelle. "The Public Fetus and the Family Car: From Abortion Politics to a Volvo Advertisement." In *Public Culture* 4, 2 (spring 1992): 67–80.

———. "Image of Contradiction: Obstetrical Ultrasound in American Culture." In *Reproducing Reproduction: Kinship, Power, and Technological Innovation*, ed. Sarah Franklin and Helena Ragoné, 15–45. Philadelphia: University of Pennsylvania Press, 1998.

Teresi, Dick, and Kathleen McAuliffe. "Male Pregnancy." In *Sex/Machine: Readings in Culture, Gender, and Technology*, ed. Patrick D. Hopkins, 175–83. Bloomington: Indiana University Press, 1998.

Thomson, Judith Jarvis. "A Defense of Abortion." In *The Problem of Abortion*, ed. Joel Feinberg, 2nd ed., 173–87. Belmont, CA: Wadsworth, 1984.

Tribe, Lawrence H. *Abortion: The Clash of Absolutes*. New York: Norton, 1992.

Tushnet, Mark. *Abortion*. Constitutional Issues Series. New York: Facts on File, 1996.

———. *Making Constitutional Law: Thurgood Marshall and the Supreme Court, 1961–1991*. New York: Oxford University Press, 1997.

U.N. Population Division. *Abortion Policies: A Global Review*. Vol. 1. New York: United Nations, 1992.

———. *Abortion Policies: A Global Review*. Vol. 2. New York: United Nations, 1993.

———. *Abortion Policies: A Global Review*. Vol. 3. New York: United Nations, 1995.

Waldron, Jeremy. "Homelessness and the Issue of Freedom." In *Contemporary Political Theory*, ed. Robert Goodin and Philip Pettit, 446–62. Oxford: Blackwell, 1997.

Warnke, Georgia. *Legitimate Differences: Interpretation in the Abortion Controversy and Other Public Debates*. Berkeley: University of California Press, 1999.

Wendell, Susan. *The Rejected Body: Feminist Philosophical Reflections on Disability*. New York: Routledge, 1996.

Wertheimer, Roger. "Understanding Blackmun's Argument." In *Abortion: Moral and Legal Perspectives*, ed. Jay L. Garfield and Patricia Hennessey, 105–22. Amherst: University of Massachusetts Press, 1984.

———. "Understanding the Abortion Argument." In *The Problem of Abortion*, ed. Joel Feinberg, 2nd ed., 43–57. Belmont, CA: Wadsworth, 1984.

West, Robin. "Liberalism and Abortion." *Georgetown Law Review* 87, 6 (June 1999): 2117–37.

Wilcox, Clyde, and Julia Riches. "Pills in the Public's Mind: RU 486 and the Framing of the Abortion Issue." Unpublished article.

Zaitchik, Alan. "Viability and the Morality of Abortion." In *The Problem of Abortion*, ed. Joel Feinberg, 2nd ed., 58–64. Belmont, CA: Wadsworth, 1984.

Index

pro-choice
  movement, 38, 39, 82
  public education project (PCPEP),
    80–82, 112, 159n. 80
pro-life
  campaign materials, 79–80, 82,
    85–88, 91–92, 100, 113, 116,
    123, 136, 157n. 64
  movement, 33, 35, 82, 88–89, 121,
    127, 135
  music, 86, 137–38, 154n. 16
public opinion, 27–28, 32, 132–33,
  146n. 93

quickening, 42, 141n. 26

Rapp, Rayna, 152n. 62
Regan, Donald, 50–59, 62, 64, 72, 75,
  77
Rhoden, Nancy, 7, 15–18, 22, 24, 26, 56
Riches, Julia, 132–33
right to life, 42, 72
Roberts, Dorothy, 37–38
Roe v. Wade
  critics of, 3, 15, 74–75
  history of, 7–12
  and its regulatory scheme, 3–5, 7,
    27, 33, 38, 48, 50, 75, 131,
    134–35
Rothman, Barbara Katz, 157n. 57
RU 486, 24, 40

Samaritanism
  and bodily impositions, 58–59
  and the law, 50–64, 66, 72, 104–5
  and time span for nontherapeutic
    abortion, 55–56, 132, 149n. 25

Sawicki, Jana, 97
Schroedel, Jean, 108–9
self defense, right of, 64–66, 70
Shapiro, Ian, 77
Sister Serpents, 108, 117–18, 160nn.
  91–92
social responsibility, 34–37, 40, 88,
  132
Solinger, Rickie, 38, 78
Sprinkle, Annie, 122–24
Stabile, Carole, 103
Steinberg, Deborah, 90–91
Stenberg, 23–24,
Sunstein, Cass, 21, 37, 44–45, 52–54,
  75

Taylor, Janelle, 97
Thomson, Judith, 59–60
Tribe, Lawrence, 20, 144n. 67
Tushnet, Mark, 13, 42

ultrasound, obstetrical, 92, 94–97,
  126
undue burden standard, 5, 27

viability, 3–40, 42, 48, 49, 133,
  139n. 2, 147n. 2

Waldron, Jeremy, 47
Warnke, Georgia, 149n. 21
Webster, 4
Wertheimer, Roger, 6, 14, 71
West, Robin, 68
Wilcox, Clyde, 132–33
Woodward, Bob, 13–14

Zaitchik, Alan, 6, 14